Spanish Kids

A Complete Guide to Understand and Speak a New Language Starting from Zero

Kids Can Learn in a Fun and Exiting Way

Cassidy Mind
Paula Delgado

**Copyright © 2020
Cassidy Mind**

All right reserved

Introduction

Welcome to "Spanish for Kids: A Complete Guide to Understand and Speak a New Language Starting from Zero – Kids Can Learn in a Fun and Exiting Way." In this book, you will find a treasure trove of information about the Spanish language. With this book, kids can quickly and easily learn Spanish. You will find that learning Spanish has never been easier.

In the following pages, you will find easy-to-follow lessons that gradually build up in the level of difficulty. Soon, kids will have the opportunity to speak a full phrase and short dialogues. This will enable them to communicate effectively without having to spend hours going through vocabulary and grammar exercises.

This volume is intended for anyone who wants to learn Spanish quickly and effectively. No prior knowledge of Spanish is needed. Thus, this book is ideal for anyone who is just starting out. All you need is the willingness to spend time on each lesson. In general, devoting a few minutes a day is a great way to get started learning this amazing language. There is no need to spend hours on end.

Each lesson has been designed to last about 30 to 45 minutes. As such, they are a quick and easy way to get started with Spanish.

Additionally, each of the lessons contains a Spanish-language text along with its corresponding English version. This facilitates comprehension by helping learners see the language in action. Also, it avoids creating confusion when words or phrases are new. As a result, there is no stress when it comes to learning.

To start off, we will provide an overview of the Spanish language. We'll be looking at its grammatical structure, pronunciation, and main features. This will lay the groundwork for the most important components of the language. Then, we will be looking at individual topics such as colors, shapes, and actions. Consequently, learners will get an easy introduction to the vocabulary and grammar used in Spanish.

Speaking of grammar, this book does not contain boring grammar lessons. Grammar is taught in context. This means that learners can expect to see grammar in the way it's meant to be used.

Therefore, there are not long, complex grammatical explanations. The point here is to use the language in context right away. This will not only facilitate learning but also make it more enjoyable.

Also, grammar is taught deductively in this book. This approach provides students with the opportunity to build their own knowledge. As a result, students can internalize grammatical structures in a way that makes sense to them. This is an intuitive process that leads to greater understanding and retention of the material.

So, let's get started learning this amazing language. Learners of all ages can take the material contained herein to develop their skills in short order. As such, there is no need to struggle with complex materials and grammar dissection. Everything you need to know is right here. This book will serve as the cornerstone of your Spanish skills.

All it takes is focused practice a few minutes at a time. Before you know it, you'll be done with this book.

Let me know what you think of the book. Your review on Amazon is welcome! Come on, then! Let's get started right now.

TABLE OF CONTENTS

Introduction	3
Chapter 1	**7**
Spanish 101	8
Inner Workings of Spanish	8
Grammar Tenses	9
False Friends	10
Articles	11
Chapter 2	**13**
Spanish Grammar	14
The verb "To Be"	14
Verb Conjugation in the Present Simple	17
Verb Conjugation in the Past	19
Verb conjugation in the future simple	21
Chapter 3	**23**
Spanish Pronunciation	24
Spanish Vowel Sounds	24
Spanish Consonant Sounds	25
Letter Combinations in Spanish	29
Final Thoughts About Pronunciation	31
Chapter 4	**32**
Los Colores	33
Acertijos (Riddles)	36
Soluciones (Solutions)	37
Chapter 5	**39**
Los Números	40
Acertijos (Riddles)	44
Soluciones (Solutions)	46
Chapter 6	**49**
Los Días de la Semana	50
Acertijos (Riddles)	53
Soluciones (Solutions)	54
Chapter 7	**56**
La Ropa	57
Acertijos (Riddles)	60
Soluciones (Solutions)	62
Chapter 8	**65**
La Escuela	66
Acertijos (Riddles)	70
Soluciones (Solutions)	71
Chapter 9	**72**
La Familia	73
Acertijos (Riddles)	76
Soluciones (Solutions)	78
Chapter 10	**80**
Los Juego	81
Acertijos (Riddles)	85
Soluciones (Solutions)	86
Chapter 11	**88**
Me Gusta Ir a la Escuela	89
El presente simple (The present simple)	93
Acertijos (Riddles)	95
Soluciones (Solutions)	96
Chapter 12	**98**
Estoy Leyendo un Libro	99
El present continuo (The present continuous)	103

Acertijos (Riddles)	104
Soluciones (Solutions)	105
Chapter 13	**107**
Mi Cumpleaños Fue Ayer	108
El pretérito perfecto simple (The past simple)	112
Acertijos (Riddles)	113
Soluciones (Solutions)	114
Chapter 14	**116**
Tuvimos Unas Grandes Vacaciones	117
El pretérito imperfecto (The indefinite past)	121
Acertijos (Riddles)	122
Soluciones (Solutions)	124
Chapter 15	**126**
Seré un Astronauta	127
El future simple (The future simple)	131
Acertijos (Riddles)	132
Soluciones (Solutions)	133
Conclusion	**134**

Chapter 1
Capítulo Uno

Spanish 101

Spanish belongs to the family of Romance languages. This family of languages receives this name as its linguistic roots are found in Latin, the language of the ancient Roman Empire. The Romance language family includes French, Italian, and Portuguese. This family is relatively small, especially when compared to other linguistic families.

Spanish emerged from what is known as the "Iberian Peninsula." This area comprises Spain and Portugal today. While there are many other languages spoken in the Iberian Peninsula, Spanish is the predominant language in Spain.

Over the centuries, Spanish has had several significant influences. Spanish began as a local dialect spoken by the inhabitants of central Spain. Then, the control of the Roman Empire led to a merge between Latin and this local dialect. From here, old Spanish was formed. This version was then influenced by the Moor Conquest. The Moors were people from northern Africa that controlled the Iberian Peninsula after the Romans were defeated. After about eight centuries of occupation, the Moors left the Iberian Peninsula.

Since the 14th century, Spanish has gone through several transformations as it spread throughout the world. Mainly, the Spanish conquest of America led to the dissemination of this language throughout what is known as Latin America today. Latin American nations have Spanish as their main language. As a result, there are roughly 500 million native speakers of Spanish in Central and South America. The only notable exception is Brazil as its main language is Portuguese.

Inner Workings of Spanish

Since Spanish is a Romance language, its grammatical system differs from that of English. There are notable differences that make it quite different from English. So, let's look at them.

- **Gender**. Like all Romance languages, the masculine and feminine gender is assigned to all nouns. Therefore, it can be tricky to know which nouns masculine and which ones are are feminine. Generally speaking, nouns ending in an "o" are masculine while nouns ending in an "a" are feminine.

Many personal pronouns in Spanish express gender: él/ella (he/she), but also nosotros/nosotras (we, masculine/feminine), vosotros/vosotras (you, plural masculine/feminine) and ellos/ellas (they, masculine/feminine). This is a stark contrast from English, as English is a gender-neutral language.

- **Plural adjectives**. Adjectives in Spanish are singular and plural. This is another significant difference from English as all adjectives are singular in English.
- **Verb conjugation**. All verbs in Spanish have a specific ending that's used to conjugate them. These endings depend on the subject and tense. The good news is that there are predictable patterns that you can easily learn.
- **Punctuation**. There are some differences in the use of punctuation. In particular, you'll find the use of diacritics atop certain vowels will help you grasp the pronunciation of specific words. Don't worry, we'll be going over this in greater detail.
- **Pronunciation**. Spanish is known as a "phonetic" language. This means that letters sound exactly like their name. This situation makes reading and pronunciation a lot easier. So, all you have to do is learn the name of the letter and off you go.

Grammar Tenses

Spanish grammar works much the same way English grammar does. The past, present, and future all used in the same way.

However, there are some differences. Mainly, the differences between English and Spanish grammar lie in the way verb tenses are structured.

In English, there is very little chance of the spelling of verb tenses. For example, verbs in the present simple are conjugated as "play" and "plays." However, In Spanish, you will find them as "juego," "jugamos," or "juegan." These conjugations are built around specific patterns. So, it's easy to remember them once you get the hang of it.

Also, it is possible to omit the use of the subject in full sentences so long as the subject is clear. Therefore, if you know exactly who you are talking about, you can omit the verb. For example, "yo como pizza" (I eat pizza) can be expressed as "como pizza" as it is clear that you are talking about "I." These cases are very common. As such, don't be surprised if you only find the verb at the start of the sentence.

Word order also tends to be different in Spanish. For instance, adjectives come after nouns. An expression like "casa blanca" (white house) is an example of the reverse order of adjectives and nouns. While these changes are not very common, it is important to note as they may cause some confusion when articulating sentences.

Lastly, please note that Spanish uses two separate verbs to mean the verb "to be." Firstly, "ser" (which translates as "to be") is used to indicate permanent states. This verb is used to describe things like name, nationality, personality, and physical characteristics. As a result, anything that is considered permanent about you must be expressed using this verb. The other verb form is "estar." This version is used to refer to anything that is considered temporary such as your current location. If you say, "estoy en casa" you are literally saying, "I am at home." This is considered a temporary state as it is quite probable that your location will change over time. So, it's important to become familiar with the verbs "ser" and "estar."

False Friends

English and Spanish have words that are very similar but have a completely different meaning. The words are called "false cognates" though they are commonly referred to as "false friends." A great example of these words is the combination "actualmente/actually." In Spanish, "actualmente" is used to mean "currently." Therefore, it has a completely different meaning than it does in English.

As you progress through your study of Spanish, you will find such words. Here is a quick list of the most common ones:

English	Correct Translation	Confused With	English Version
Actually	De hecho	Actualmente	Currently
Assist	Ayudar	Asistir	Attend
Attend	Asistir	Atender	Attend to
Carpet	Alfombra	Carpeta	Folder

Deception	Engaño	Decepción	Disappoint
Embarrassed	Avergonzado	Embarazada	Pregnant
Exit	Salida	Éxito	Success
Idiom	Modismo	Idioma	language

This list serves to illustrate how there are some words that look the same but mean different things. So, please be careful whenever you run into them. It could save you some headaches!

Articles

In English, there is one indefinite article "a/an" and one definite article "the." In Spanish, there are singular indefinite article "un" and "una" while also plural indefinite articles, "unos/unas." Please note that "un" and "unos" are masculine while "una/unas" are feminine. As for the definite article, there is "el" and "la," which are singular, while also "los/las," which are plural. "El/los" are masculine, whereas "la/las" are feminine.

Let's look at some examples.

Singular indefinite articles

- Yo tengo **un** perro pequeño y juguetón. (I have a small and playful dog.)
- María vive en **una** mansión. (María lives in a mansion.)
- José come **una** pizza vegetariana. (José eats a vegetarian pizza.)
- Marta juega con **un** balón nuevo. (Marta plays with a new ball.)

As you can see, "un" is used to refer to a singular, masculine noun. "Una" is used to refer to a singular, feminine noun.

Plural indefinite articles

- Hay **unas** flores bonitas en el patio. (There are some beautiful flowers in the yard.)
- Jorge tiene **unas** monedas antiguas. (Jorge has some antique coins.)
- Los niños corren con **unos** zapatos viejos. (The children run with some old shoes.)
- Hay **unas** nubes en el cielo. (There are some clouds in the sky.)

In these examples, we can see that "unos" (masculine, plural), and "unas" (feminine, plural) are used to mean "some." As such, it is important for you to notice if you are talking about a masculine or feminine noun.

Definite articles

Let's get a closer look at the definite articles el, la, los, and las.

- **La** casa es de color azul. (The house is blue.)
- Juan tiene **la** comida. (Juan has the food.)
- Mi papá compra **el** diario todos los días. (My father buys the newspaper every day.)
- Mi madre hace **el** almuerzo. (My mother prepares the lunch.)
- Todos **los** días son divertidos en mi escuela. (All days are fun at my school.)
- **Los** niños juegan después de clases. (The children play after school.)
- Miguel tiene **las** camisas. (Miguel has the shirts.)
- Vicky juega con **las** muñecas por la tarde. (Vicky plays with the dolls in the afternoon.)

Please note that all definite articles in Spanish translate as "the" in English. So, it's important to note the difference in terms of gender and number of nouns. As such, please make sure that you if you have a plural noun, you have the right gender.

Chapter 2
Capítulo Dos

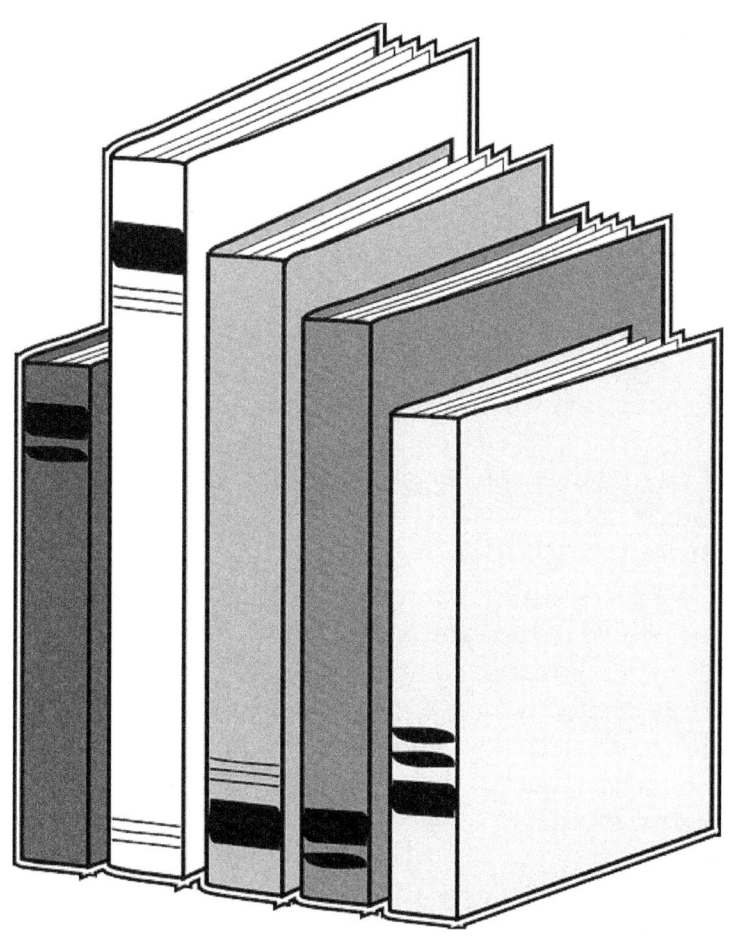

Spanish Grammar

Generally Spanish grammar works the same way as English grammar. As such, it is clear to see that the present, past and future simple are used in the same way as they are in English. The main difference lies in the way these verbs are conjugated.

So, let's look at how you can conjugate verbs in Spanish.

The verb "To Be"

The first verb we are going to conjugate is the verb "to be." Please remember there are two versions of this verb.

Let's start with "ser."

- Yo **soy** un estudiante de la escuela primaria. (I am a primary school student.)
- Tú **eres** una niña muy inteligente. (You are a very intelligent girl.)
- Él **es** un chico con muchas habilidades. (He is a kid with many skills.)
- Ella **es** una chica alta y atlética. (She is a tall and athletic kid.)
- Nosotros **somos** compañeros de la misma clase. (We are classmates in the same class.)
- Nosotras **somos** compañeras de la misma clase. (We are classmates in the same class.)
- Vosotros **sois** los mejores estudiantes. (You are the best students.)
- Vosotros **sois** las mejores estudiantes. (You are the best students.)
- Ellos **son** estudiantes de secundaria. (They are secondary school students.)
- Ellas **son** trabajadoras en una oficina. (They are workers in an office.)

Please note that "tú" means "you" while "tu" means "your." The difference lies in the use of the "tilde." The tilde is the accent placed atop vowels in Spanish. Also, "él" refers to "he" whereas "el" refers to "the."

For ease, from now on we will use only the masculine version for "nosotros y vosotros", we and you.

So, please take the time to go over these conjugations as "ser" has an irregular conjugation. However, it is one of the most important verbs in the language.

Here is a look at the conjugation of "ser" in the past.

In Spanish we find different type of past. The past simple is essentially used to talk about any action that occurred at any point. The indefinite past is used to talk about actions that were in progress at some point in the past. This means the action was happening at the time the speaker is referring to.

- Yo **fui/era** un estudiante de la escuela primaria. (I was a primary school student.)
- Tú **fuiste/eras** una niña muy inteligente. (You were a very intelligent girl.)
- Él **fue/era** un chico con muchas habilidades. (He was a kid with many skills.)
- Ella **fue/era** una chica alta y atlética. (She was a tall and athletic kid.)
- Nosotros **fuimos/éramos** compañeros de la misma clase. (We were classmates in the same class.)
- Vosotros **fuisteis/erais** los mejores estudiantes. (You were the best students.)
- Ellos **fueron/eran** estudiantes de secundaria. (They were secondary school students.)
- Ellas **fueron/eran** trabajadoras en una oficina. (They were workers in an office.)

Here is a look at ser in the future:

- Yo **serán** un estudiante de la escuela primaria. (I will be a primary school student.)
- Tú **serás** una niña muy inteligente. (You will be a very intelligent girl.)
- Él **será** un chico con muchas habilidades. (He will be a kid with many skills.)
- Ella **será** una chica alta y atlética. (She will be a tall and athletic kid.)
- Nosotros **seremos** compañeros de la misma clase. (We will be classmates in the same class.)

- Vosotros **seréis** los mejores estudiantes. (You will be the best students.)
- Ellos **serán** estudiantes de secundaria. (They will be secondary school students.)
- Ellas **serán** trabajadoras en una oficina. (They will be workers in an office.)

Now, let's take a look at "*estar*."
- Yo **estoy** dentro de mi auto. (I am inside my car.)
- Tú **estás** con el perro. (You are with the dog.)
- Él **está** afuera de la escuela. (He is outside of school.)
- Ella **está** con su nueva compañera de clases. (She is with her new classmate.)
- Nosotros **estamos** acá. (We are here.)
- Vosotros **estáis** con sus mascotas. (You are with your pets.)
- Ellos **están** en sus habitaciones. (They are in their rooms.)
- Ellas **están** en el salón de belleza. (They are at the beauty salon.)

In this case, we can see the conjugation differs somewhat. "Yo," "tú," and "nosotros" have different conjugations while "él/ella," and "ellos/ellas" have the same verb conjugation, respectively.

Here is "estar" in the past.
- Yo **estuve/estaba** dentro de mi auto. (I was inside my car.)
- Tú **estuviste/estabas** con el perro. (You were with the dog.)
- Él **estuvo/estaba** afuera de la escuela. (He was outside of school.)
- Ella **estuvo/estaba** con su nueva compañera de clases. (She was with her new classmate.)
- Nosotros **estuvimos/estábamos** acá. (We were here.)
- Vosotros **estuvieron/estabais** con sus mascotas. (You were with your pets.)
- Ellos **estuvieron/estaban** en sus habitaciones. (They were in their rooms.)
- Ellas **estuvieron/estaban** en el salón de belleza. (They were at the beauty salon.)

Here is "estar" in the future.
- Yo **estaré** dentro de mi auto. (I will be inside my car.)

- Tú **estarás** con el perro. (You will be with the dog.)
- Él **estará** afuera de la escuela. (He will be outside of school.)
- Ella **estará** con su nueva compañera de clases. (She will be with her new classmate.)
- Nosotros **estaremos** acá. (We will be here.)
- Vosotros **estaréis** con sus mascotas. (You will be with your pets.)
- Ellos **estarán** en sus habitaciones. (They will be in their rooms.)
- Ellas **estarán** en el salón de belleza. (They will be at the beauty salon.)

Verb Conjugation in the Present Simple

To begin with, it's important to consider the endings of infinitive verbs in Spanish. The infinitive form of the verb is the one before its conjugation.

The three endings of infinitive verbs in Spanish are ER, AR, and IR. Let's look at some examples:

ER ending
- Comer (to eat)
- Correr (to run)
- Barrer (to sweep)

IR ending
- Dormir (to sleep)
- Abrir (to open)
- Sentir (to feel)

AR ending
- Saltar (to jump)
- Jugar (to play)
- Caminar (to walk)

Now, let's look at some sample conjugations.

Verb: Correr (to run)
- Yo **corro** en la escuela todos los días. (I run at school every day.)

- Tú **corres** en la calle por las mañanas. (You run on the street every morning.)
- Él **corre** cada fin de semana. (He runs every weekend.)
- Ella **corre** con sus perros. (She runs with her dogs.)
- Nosotros **corremos** con nuestros amigos. (We run with our friends.)
- Vosotros **corréis** para hacer ejercicio. (You run to do exercise.)
- Ellos **corren** en el campo. (They run on the field.)
- Ellas **corren** todo el tiempo. (They run all the time.)

Please note that all you need to do is drop the ER ending and replace it with the corresponding ending based on the subject.

Here is a breakdown:
- Yo – o
- Tú – es
- Él – e
- Ella – e
- Nosotros – emos
- Vosotros – eis
- Ellos – en
- Ellas – en

As you can see, there is a recurring pattern that you can apply to all verbs ending in ER.

Now, let's look at verbs ending in AR. The pattern is quite similar to verbs ending in ER. There is just a slight difference.

Verb: Saltar (to jump)
- Yo **salto** en el gimnasio. (I jump at the gym.)
- Tú **saltas** en casa. (You jump at home.)
- Él **salta** en el trabajo. (He jumps at work.)
- Ella **salta** con los niños. (She jumps with the children.)
- Nosotros **saltamos** juntos. (We jump together.)
- Vosotros **saltais** en el parque. (You jump at the park.)
- Ellos **saltan** solos. (They jump by themselves.)
- Ellas **saltan** con energía. (They jump with energy.) Here is the breakdown of the endings.
- Yo – o
- Tú – as
- Él – a

- Ella – a
- Nosotros – amos
- Vosotros – ais
- Ellos – an
- Ellas – an

Please note that instead of having an "e" precede the endings, it is an "a."

Let's take a look at verbs ending in IR. The endings for these verbs differ somewhat from the previous two.

Verb: Abrir (to open)
- Yo **abro** la puerta de la casa. (I open the house's door.)
- Tú **abres** la puerta del auto. (You open the car's door.)
- Él **abre** la lata. (He opens the can.)
- Ella **abre** el sobre. (She opens the envelope.)
- Nosotros **abrimos** la caja. (We open the box.)
- Vosotros **abrís** el paquete. (You open the package.)
- Ellos **abren** los libros. (They open the books.)
- Ellas **abren** las bolsas. (They open the bags.) Here is the breakdown:
- Yo – o
- Tú – es
- Él – e
- Ella – e
- Nosotros – imos
- Vosotros – is
- Ellos – en
- Ellas – en

In general, the pattern is the same. There is only two slight changes in the pattern, particularly with "imos" and "is". Otherwise, the conjugation for verbs ending in IR is essentially the same.

Verb Conjugation in the Past

Verb conjugation of the past works the same way as in the present simple. There is a series of verb endings that correspond to the infinitive ending.

So, let's jump right in!

Verb: Correr (to run)
- Yo **corrí/corría** en la escuela todos los días. (I ran at school every day.)
- Tú **corriste/corrías** en la calle por las mañanas. (You ran on the street every morning.)
- Él **corrió/corría** cada fin de semana. (He ran every weekend.)
- Ella **corrió/corría** con sus perros. (She ran with her dogs.)
- Nosotros **corrimos/corríamos** con nuestros amigos. (We ran with our friends.)
- Vosotros **corristeis/corríais** para hacer ejercicio. (You ran to do exercise.)
- Ellos **corrieron/corrían** en el campo. (They ran on the field.)
- Ellas **corrieron/corrían** todo el tiempo. (They ran all the time.)

Now, let's move on to an AR ending verb.

Verb: Saltar (to jump)
- Yo **salté/saltaba** en el gimnasio. (I jumped at the gym.)
- Tú **saltaste/saltabas** en casa. (You jumped at home.)
- Él **saltó/saltaba** en el trabajo. (He jumped at work.)
- Ella **saltó/saltaba** con los niños. (She jumped with the children.)
- Nosotros **saltamos/saltábamos** juntos. (We jumped together.)
- Vosotros **saltasteis/saltabais** en el parque. (You jumped at the park.)
- Ellos **saltaron/saltaban** solos. (They jumped by themselves.)
- Ellas **saltaron/saltaban** con energía. (They jumped with energy.)

Let's take a look at verbs ending in IR. The endings for these verbs differ somewhat from the previous two.

Verb: Abrir (to open)

- Yo **abrí/abría** la puerta de la casa. (I opened the house's door.)
- Tú **abriste/abrías** la puerta del auto. (You opened the car's door.)
- Él **abrió/abría** la lata. (He opened the can.)
- Ella **abrió/abría** el sobre. (She opened the envelope.)
- Nosotros **abrimos/ abríamos** la caja. (We opened the box.)
- Vosotros **abristeis/abríais** el paquete. (You opened the package.)
- Ellos **abrieron/abrían** los libros. (They opened the books.)
- Ellas **abrieron/abrían** las bolsas. (They opened the bags.)

Verb conjugation in the future simple

Here is a look at the verb conjugation for the same types of verbs in the future.

Verb: Correr (to run)
- Yo **correré** en la escuela todos los días. (I will run at school every day.)
- Tú **correrás** en la calle por las mañanas. (You will run on the street every morning.)
- Él **correrá** cada fin de semana. (He will run every weekend.)
- Ella **correrá** con sus perros. (She will run with her dogs.)
- Nosotros **correremos** con nuestros amigos. (We will run with our friends.)
- Vosotros **correréis** para hacer ejercicio. (You will run to do exercise.)
- Ellos **correrán** en el campo. (They will run on the field.)
- Ellas **correrán** todo el tiempo. (They will run all the time.)

Verb: Saltar (to jump)
- Yo **saltaré** en el gimnasio. (I will jump at the gym.)
- Tú **saltarás** en casa. (You will jump at home.)
- Él **saltará** en el trabajo. (He will jump at work.)
- Ella **saltará** con los niños. (She will jump with the children.)
- Nosotros **saltaremos** juntos. (We will jump together.)
- Vosotros **saltaréis** en el parque. (You will jump at the park.)
- Ellos **saltarán** solos. (They will jump by themselves.)
- Ellas **saltarán** con energía. (They will jump with energy.)

Verb: Abrir (to open)
- Yo **abriré** la puerta de la casa. (I will open the house's door.)
- Tú **abrirás** la puerta del auto. (You will open the car's door.)
- Él **abrirá** la lata. (He will open the can.)
- Ella **abrirá** el sobre. (She will open the envelope.)
- Nosotros **abriremos** la caja. (We will open the box.)
- Vosotros **abriréis** el paquete. (You will open the package.)
- Ellos **abrirán** los libros. (They will open the books.)
- Ellas **abrirán** las bolsas. (They will open the bags.)

With this guide, you can now confidently conjugate verbs in the Spanish language!

Chapter 3
Capítulo Tres

Spanish Pronunciation

Spanish is known as a "phonetic" language. This means that the sounds produced by letters are exactly the same as their names. As such, all you need to do is learn the individual sounds of each letter and then combine them to form sounds and words.

The Spanish alphabet uses the same character set in the English alphabet. However, there is an additional letter known as the "ñ" (en – yeh). This is the only consonant that has a diacritic above it. Other than that, all the remaining letters are basically the same as English. Their pronunciation changes slightly.

The main difference in terms of letters lies with vowels. The pronunciation of vowels is slightly different. This may cause some confusion, especially if this is your first time with English.

Nevertheless, Spanish vowels are essentially limited to five individual sounds.

So, let's take a look at Spanish vowel sounds.

Spanish Vowel Sounds

Generally speaking, vowel sounds are produced with little to no restriction of airflow. This means that the mouth is open with the tongue mainly in a flat position. The difference in sound is the result of lips and mouth placement. So, you must be aware of how to articulate each sound.

In Spanish, there are five vowel sounds.

- A -- /ah/
- E -- /eh/
- I -- /eeh/
- -- /oh/
- U -- /ooh/
- ☐ Please keep in mind that Spanish vowels are not rounded as they are in English. Thus, they produce a "flatter" sound than in English. The difference in pronunciation among vowels is what greatly distinguishes Spanish from English pronunciation.
- ☐ Let's have a look at some examples.
- Antes -- /ahn – tehs/ (before)
- Amigo -- /ah – meeh – goh/ (friend)

- Planta -- /plahn – tah/ (plant)
- Eso -- /eh – soh/ (that)
- Lente -- /lehn – teh/ (lens)
- Mente -- /mehn – teh/ (mind)
- Lindo -- /leehn – doh/ (nice)
- Tinta -- /teehn – tah/ (ink)
- Pintar -- /peehn – tahr/ (paint)
- Monto -- /mohn – toh/ (amount)
- Hoyo -- /oh – yoh/ (hole)
- Botón -- /boh – tohn/ (button)
- Musa -- /mooh – sah/ (muse)
- Luna /loohn – nah/ (moon)
- Puma /pooh – mah/ (cougar)

These examples highlight how vowel sounds remain the same regardless of their placement in a word. So, please take the time to go over their pronunciation so that you can become familiar with them.

Now, let's move on to consonant sounds.

Spanish Consonant Sounds

Consonant sounds in Spanish are straightforward. Once you get the hang of them, it is easy to pronounce them. The most notable exception is "h" as it is silent. Therefore, you must never pronounce this letter regardless of its positioning in a word. It can be a bit tricky to know which words must be spelled with an "h," but you'll quickly get the hang of it.

Here are the Spanish consonants:
- B -- /beh/
- C -- /seh/
- D -- /deh/
- F -- /eh – feh/
- G -- /heh/
- H -- /ah – cheh/
- J -- /hoh – tah/
- K -- /kah/
- L -- /eh – leh/

25

- M -- /eh – meh/
- N -- /eh – neh/
- Ñ -- /ehn – yeh/
- P -- /peh/
- Q -- /kooh/
- R -- /eh – reh/
- S -- /eh – seh/
- T -- /teh/
- V -- /veh/
- W -- /doh – bleh – veh/
- X -- /eh – kees/
- Y -- /eeh – greeh - eh – gah/
- Z -- /zeh – tah/

Let's take a look at some examples for each letter.
- B
  - Base /bah – seh/ (base)
  - Balón /bah – lohn/ (ball)
  - Bebé /beh – beh/ (baby)
- D
  - Día /deeh – ah/ (day)
  - Dedo /deh – doh/ (finger)
  - Dona /doh – nah/ (donut)
- F
  - Fin /feehn/ (end)
  - Fondo /fohn – doh/ (bottom)
  - Feria /feh – reeh – ah/ (fair)
- G
  - Gato /gah – toh/ (cat)
  - Goma /goh – mah/ (glue)
  - Gusto /goohs – toh) (taste)
  - Gente /hehn – teh/ (people)
  - Giro /heeh – roh/ (turn)
- Please note that the combination GA, GO, GU all sound the same as in English. The combinations GE and GI sound like /h/ in English. However, the combinations "GUE"
- /geh/ and "GUI" /geeh/ sound differently when a "U" is

26

- added to it. For example, "guerra" /geh – rah/ and "guía"
- /geeh – ah/ sounds similar to English.
- H
  - Honor /oh – nohr/ (honor)
  - Hora /oh – rah/ (hour)
  - Honesto /oh – nehs – toh/ (honest)
- J
  - Justo /hoohs – toh/ (fair)
  - Justicia /hoohs – teeh – seeh – ah/ (justice)
  - Jarra /hah – rah/ (jar)
- K
  - Kilómetro /keeh – loh – meh – troh/ (kilometer)
  - Koala (same as English)
  - Kiwi (same as English)
  - Please note that "K" is seldom used in Spanish. It's mainly
  - seen in imported words.
- L
  - Limón /leeh – mohn/ (lime)
  - Lento /lehn – toh/ (slow)
  - Lana /lah – nah/ (wool)
- M
  - Mono /moh – noh/ (monkey)
  - Mar /mahr/ (sea)
  - Mula /mooh – lah/ (mule)
- N
  - Niño /neehn – yoh/ (child)
  - Nube /nooh – beh/ (cloud)
  - Nada /nah – dah/ (nothing)
- Ñ
  - Uña /oohn – yah/
  - Moño /mohn – yoh/ (bow)
  - Ñame /nyah – meh/ (yam)
- P
  - Papá /pah – pah/ (father)
  - Pista /peesh – tah/ (track)
  - Poner /poh – nehr/ (to place)

- Q
  - Queso /keh – soh/ (cheese)
  - Quinto /keehn – toh/ (fifth)
  - Querer /keh -rehr/ (to want)
- R
  - Rojo /roh – hoh/ (red)
  - Rima /reeh – mah/ (rhyme)
  - Ropa /roh – pah/ (clothes)
- S
  - Santo /sahn – toh/ (saint)
  - Salir /sah – leehr/ (to exit)
  - Subir /sooh – beehr/ (to climb)
- T
  - Tanto /tahn – toh/ (much)
  - Tonto /tohn – toh/ (silly)
  - Tela /teh – lah/ (cloth)
- V
  - Vino /veeh – noh/ (wine)
  - Volcán /vohl – kahn/ (volcano)
  - Vista /veehs – tah/ (view)
  - Please note that in Latin American Spanish, "V" is pronounced the same as "B". In European Spanish, "V" is pronounced exactly the same as in English. So, Latin American speakers would say "vino" as /beeh noh/ whereas European speakers would say /veeh – noh/.
- W
  - Wafle /wah – fleh/ (waffle)
  - Web (same as English)
  - Show (same as English)
  - Please note that "W" is seldom used in Spanish. It's mainly seen in imported words.
- X
  - Éxito /ehk – seeh – toh/ (success)
  - Texto /tehks – toh/ (text)
  - Sexto /sehks – toh/ (sixth)
- Y

- Yunque /yoonh – kehn/ (anvil)
- Yate /yah – teh/ (yacht)
- Ley /lehy/ (law)
- Please note that "Y" at the end of the word adds the /ay/ sound as in "high."
- Z
  - Zumo /zooh – moh/ (juice)
  - Azúcar /ah – zooh – kahr/ (sugar)
  - Cazar /kah – zahr/ (to hunt)
  - Please note that in Latin American Spanish, "Z" sounds exactly the same as "S". In European Spanish, "Z" sounds like /th/ in English. For example, "corazón" would sound more like /koh – rah – thon/.

Letter Combinations in Spanish

As with all languages, some letter combinations break the main phonetic rules of the language. Let's take a look at them.

- CE, CI
  - This letter combination sounds as /seh/ and /seeh/. Here are some examples:
  - Cine -- /seeh – neh/ (cinema)
  - Cincho /seehn – choh/ (belt)
  - Cena -- /seh – nah/ (dinner)
  - Cerrar -- /seh – rahr/ (to close)
- LL
- RR
  - The "LL" combination sounds as /y/. For instance:
  - Llorar -- /yoh – rahr/ (to cry)

- Lluvia -- /yooh – veeh – ah/ (rain)
- Llanta -- /yahn – tah/ (tire)
- Tallo -- /tah – yoh/ (stem)

- CH
  - This letter combination sounds the same as English.
  - Chocar /choh – kahr/ (to crash)
  - Ocho /oh – choh/ (eight)
  - Apachar /ah – pah – chahr/ (to press)

- R
  - This is the hard, rolling /r/ sound in Spanish. It can be a bit tough to master. All it takes is the tip of your tongue to vibrate as you keep it flat, behind your upper front teeth. Here are some examples:
  - Perro -- /peh – roh/ (dog)
  - Carro -- /kah – roh/ (car)
  - Burro -- /booh – roh/ (donkey)

- SH
  - This combination isn't native to Spanish. It has been imported from other languages. For example, "show" or "flash" sounds exactly the same as in English.
  - However, you need to be careful as there are plenty of words that use this combination but produce the sounds separately as the "h" is silent. Here are some examples:
  - Deshacer /dehs – ah – sehr/ (undo)
  - Deshonra /dehs – ohn – rah/ (dishonor)

- Deshielo /dehs – eeh – eh – loh) (thaw)

Final Thoughts About Pronunciation

As you can see, Spanish pronunciation is very straightforward. You can quite easily begin sounding out words without having to guess at how they sound. Of course, getting the right pronunciation takes some time and practice. Still, you can make the most of your efforts by focusing on the tips in this guide.

If you are ever in doubt regarding pronunciation, there are free, online tools that you can use. First, Google has a great translation and pronunciation tool that you can use to help you get the right sounds. Also, the tool www.spanishdict.com is a great way to help you navigate the waters of Spanish pronunciation.

At this point, we are now ready to begin on the journey of learning Spanish vocabulary in real-life stories. So, let's get started. We are going to have a blast!

Chapter 4
Capítulo Cuatro

Los Colores

Important words to remember:

Español	English	Pronunciation
rojo	red	/roh – hoh/
azul	blue	/ah – zoohl/
amarillo	yellow	/ah – mah – reeh – yoh/
verde	green	/vehr – deh/
naranja	orange	/nah – rahn – hah/
morado	purple	/moh – rah -doh/
blanco	white	/blahn – koh/
rosa	pink	/roh – sah/
marrón	brown	/mah – rohn/
negro	black	/neh – groh/

Los Colores (The Colors)

Español	English
Juan tiene ocho años. Él está muy emocionado porque pronto es su cumpleaños. Él quiere una gran fiesta con todos sus amigos. El papá de Juan tiene mucho que hacer. Debe realizar todos los preparativos para la fiesta. En total, Juan espera a casi cincuenta	Juan is eight years old. He is very excited because his birthday is coming soon. He wants a big party with all his friends. Juan's father has a lot to do. He must make all the preparations for the party. In all, Juan expects almost fifty of his friends and classmates from school.
de sus amigos y compañeros de la escuela.	Juan's mother is very busy with the preparations. She

La madre de Juan está muy ocupada con los preparativos. Ella prepara la comida y las decoraciones. En esta fiesta, Juan quiere impresionar a sus amigos. Por eso, la madre de Juan prepara las decoraciones más especiales. Ella prepara una sorpresa para todos los amigos y compañeros de Juan. Las decoraciones son de color **rojo** y **azul**.

La fiesta será dentro de una semana. Juan no puede dormir de la emoción. Todos los días se encuentra emocionado con la idea de su fiesta. Su madre hace todo lo necesario para la fiesta de Juan.

Pero Juan no puede esperar más. Es un niño inquieto. Todos los días la pregunta a su madre si todo está listo. Cada vez que Juan la pregunta a su madre ella le responde que las decoraciones tienen muchos colores como **amarillo**, **verde**, y **naranja**.

El padre de Juan también debe realizar muchos preparativos. El padre de Juan es el encargado del pastel. El pastel de cumpleaños es algo espectacular. Pero también es una sorpresa. Nadie sabe cómo es. Solamente el padre de Juan sabe el secreto. Juan no puede esperar más para ver su pastel. Él necesita saber cómo es su pastel... ¡ya!

El día de la gran fiesta está aquí.

prepares the food and decorations. At this party, Juan wants to impress his friends. For this reason, Juan's mother prepares the most special decorations. She prepares a surprise for all of Juan's friends and colleagues. The decorations are **red** and **blue**.

The party will be in a week. Juan cannot sleep from emotion. Every day he is excited about the idea of his party. His mother does everything necessary for Juan's party. But Juan can't wait any longer. He is a restless child. Every day he asks his mother if everything is ready. Every time Juan asks his mother, she replies that the decorations have many colors like **yellow**, **green**, and **orange**.

Juan's father also has to make a lot of preparations. Juan's father is in charge of the cake. The birthday cake is something spectacular. But it is also a surprise. Nobody knows what it is like. Only Juan's father knows the secret. Juan can't wait any longer to see his cake. He needs to know what his cake is like... now!

Juan está super emocionado. Juan está desesperado por sus amigos. No encuentra las horas para iniciar su fiesta. Él quiere comer pastel, jugar juegos, y abrir regalos, muchos regalos. Juan está impaciente por el inicio de su fiesta. Poco a poco, sus amigos llegan a su casa. Cada uno de ellos le entrega un pequeño regalo. Unos regalos tienen moño **morado** y otros tienen un listón **blanco**. Uno de los regalos viene en una caja **rosa**. Juan está contento con sus regalos, pero hay algo más importante... ¡el pastel! De repente, la puerta se abre. Juan mira hacia el centro del jardín de su casa. Ahí entra su padre con el pastel de cumpleaños más grande del mundo. El pastel tiene forma de arcoíris. ¡Tiene todos los colores! Tiene los colores, **rojo**, **verde**, **amarillo**, **naranja**, **azul**, **rosa**, **marrón**, **blanco**, **morado**, y hasta puntitos **negros**. Los puntitos negros son chispas de chocolate. Es un pastel tan impresionante. Todos los niños en la fiesta se quedan en silencio. Es una maravilla de pastel. Es increíble ver ese pastel tan hermoso. Todos los niños quieren un trozo. Pero, primero deben cantarle feliz cumpleaños a Juan. Los niños hacen una rueda alrededor de	The day of the big party is here. Juan is super excited. Juan is impatient to see his friends. You can't find the hours to start your party. He wants to eat cake, play games, and open presents, lots of presents. Juan is impatient for the start of his party. Little by little, his friends come to his house. Each of them gives you a small gift. Some gifts have a **purple** bow and others have a **white** ribbon. One of the gifts comes in a **pink** box. Juan is happy with his gifts, but there is something more important... the cake! Suddenly the door opens. Juan looks towards the center of the garden in his house. That's where her father comes in with the biggest birthday cake in the world. The cake is shaped like a rainbow. It has all the colors! It has the colors **red**, **green**, **yellow**, **orange**, **blue**, **pink**, **brown**, **white**, **purple**, and even little **black** dots. The little black dots are chocolate chips. It's such an awesome cake. All the children at the party are silent. It is a wonder of cake. It's amazing to see such a beautiful cake. All children want a piece. But first, they must sing happy birthday to Juan. The children

Juan. Gritan con felicidad y alegría. La fiesta es alucinante. El pastel es de lo mejor. Juan recibe el trozo más grande. Los demás niños también reciben un trozo grande. El pastel está delicioso. A todos les encanta. ¡Qué día tan especial!	make a wheel around Juan. They scream with happiness and joy. The party is amazing. The cake is the best. Juan receives the largest piece. The other children also receive a large piece. The cake is delicious. Everyone loves it. What a special day!

Acertijos (Riddles)

Ejercicio número uno (exercise number one):

Coloca las letras en el orden correcto (Place the letters in the correct order).

1. lazu _____

2. ojro _____

3. nmraró _____

4. conlab _____

5. erdve _____

6. lolriama _____

7. orgen _____

8. jaranan _____

9. doraom _____

10. osra _____

Ejercicio número dos (exercise number two):

Combina la palabra en español con la palabra en inglés. (Match the Spanish word with the correct English word).

1. rojo	( ) blue
2. verde	( ) red
3. amarillo	( ) black

4. morado	( ) purple
5. blanco	( ) green
6. negro	( ) white
7. rosa	( ) orange
8. naranja	( ) brown
9. marron	( ) yellow
10. azul	( ) pink

Soluciones (Solutions)

Ejercicio número uno (exercise number one):
Coloca las letras en el orden correcto. (Place the letters in the correct order).
1. lazu **azul**
2. ojro **rojo**
3. nmraró **marrón**
4. conlab **blanco**
5. erdve **verde**
6. lolriama **amarillo**
7. orgen **negro**
8. jaranan **naranja**
9. doraom **morado**
10. osra **rosa**

Ejercicio número dos (exercise number two):
Combina la palabra en español con la palabra en inglés. (Match the Spanish word with the correct English word).

1. rojo	(10) blue
2. verde	(1) red
3. amarillo	(6) black
4. morado	(4) purple
5. blanco	(2) green
6. negro	(5) white
7. rosa	(8) orange
8. naranja	(9) brown
9. marron	(3) yellow
10. azul	(7) pink

Chapter 5
Capítulo Cinco

Los Números

Important words to remember:

Español	English	Pronunciation
uno	one	/ooh – noh/
dos	two	/dohs/
tres	three	/trehs/
cuatro	four	/kwah – troh/
cinco	five	/seehn – koh/
seis	six	/seh – eeh – ehys/
siete	seven	/seeh – eh – teh/
ocho	eight	/oh – choh/
nueve	nine	/nooh – eh – veh/
diez	ten	/deeh – ehz/
once	eleven	/ohn – seh/
doce	twelve	/doh – seh/
trece	thirteen	/treh – seh/
catorce	fourteen	/kah – tohr – seh/
quince	fifteen	/keehn– seh/
dieciséis	sixteen	/deeh – eh – seeh – seyhs/
diecisiete	seventeen	/deeh – eh – seeh – seeh - eh– seh/
dieciocho	eighteen	/deeh – ehs – eeh – oh – choh/

diecinueve	nineteen	/deeh – ehs – eeh – noo – eh – veh/
veinte	twenty	/veh – eeh – ehn – teh/
treinta	thirty	/treh – eeh – ehn - tah/
cuarenta	forty	/kwah – rehn – tah/
cincuenta	fifty	/seehn – kooh – ehn – tah/
sesenta	sixty	/seh – sehn – tah/
setenta	seventy	/seh – tehn – tah/
ochenta	eighty	/oh – chen – tah/
noventa	ninety	/noh – vehn – tah/
cien	one hundred	/seeh – ehn/

Los Números (The Numbers)

Español	English

En la escuela, los niños reciben sus clases de ciencias naturales. En este día, los niños estudian sobre los animales. La maestra les pregunta a todos los niños qué saben sobre los insectos. Algunos niños saben mucho. Otros niños saben poco.
  Pero eso no importa. Lo importante es participar en la clase.
  Durante la clase, la maestra les pide a los niños salir al patio. En el patio, ellos observan las plantas, los árboles, las aves y los insectos.
  María, una niña muy inteligente, levanta su mano. Ella comienza a
	At school, the children take their natural science classes. On this day, children study about animals. The teacher asks all the children what they know about insects. Some children know a lot. Other children know little. But that does not matter. The important thing is to participate in the class.
	  During class, the teacher asks the children to go outside. In the yard, they observe plants, trees, birds, and insects. Maria, a very smart girl, raises her hand. She

hablar sobre las hormigas. María les dice a sus compañeros que tiene	starts talking about ants. Maria tells her classmates that

muchas hormigas en su casa. Las hormigas hacen una fila en donde se llevan todo lo que encuentran.

La maestra felicita a María. Luego, les pide a los demás niños que hablen sobre los insectos. Pedro levanta su mano. Él comienza a describir las abejas que viven cerca de su casa. Los compañeros de Pedro ponen mucha atención. Ellos les tienen miedo a las abejas. Pero las abejas no son malas porque producen miel.

Los niños y la maestra continúan caminando por el patio de la escuela. De pronto, encuentran un hormiguero. Un hormiguero es un lugar en donde viven las hormigas. Ellas cavan un hoyo en la tierra. De ahí entran y salen con su comida. Los niños están impresionados con el hormiguero.Ahora, la maestra les pide a los niños contar las hormigas. Entonces, los niños comienzan... **uno**, **dos**, **tres**, **cuatro**, **cinco**, **seis**, **siete**, **ocho**, **nueve**... y **diez**. Pero son muchas, muchas hormigas. Son negras, y corren muy rápido. Así que deben apurarse para continuar contando.

Once, **doce**, **trece**, **catorce**, **quince**, **dieciséis**, **diecisiete**, **dieciocho**, **diecinueve**, **veinte**.

¡Los niños cuentan veinte hormigas!

she has a lot of ants in her house. The ants line up where they take everything they find.

The teacher congratulates Maria. Then she asks the other children to talk about the insects. Pedro raises his hand. He begins to describe the bees that live near his house. Pedro's classmates pay close attention. They are afraid of bees. But bees are not bad because they produce honey.

The children and the teacher continue to walk around the schoolyard. Suddenly, they find an anthill. An anthill is a place where ants live. They dig a hole in the ground. From there they go in and out with their food. The children are impressed with the anthill.

Now the teacher asks the children to count the ants. So, the children start... one, two, three, four, five, six, seven, eight, nine... and ten. But there are many, many ants.
They are black, and they run very fast. So, they must hurry to continue counting.

Eleven, **twelve**, **thirteen**, **fourteen**, **fifteen**, **sixteen**, **seventeen**, **eighteen**, **nineteen**, **twenty**.

Pero hay más... muchas más...

Los niños siguen contando, una por una... **veintiuno**... **veintidós**... **veintitrés**... **veinticuatro**... **veinticinco**... **veintiséis**... **veintisiete**... **veintiocho**... **veintinueve**... **treinta**.

Pero hay más... muchas más...

Treinta... **cuarenta**... **cincuenta**... **sesenta**... **setenta**... **ochenta**... **noventa**... y ¡**cien**!

¡Hay **cien** hormigas!

¿De dónde salen tantas hormigas? Hay hormigas por doquier.

Los niños saben que existen muchas hormigas dentro de un hormiguero. Pero la maestra les indica que es hora de regresar al aula. Es hora de continuar con las demás clases. Contar hormigas es divertido, pero las demás clases también son divertidas. Aún hay mucho por aprender.

La escuela es un lugar divertido. Es divertido aprender sobre muchas cosas. Los niños son felices de aprender tantas cosas sobre el mundo. Ahora toca la clase de matemáticas. Los niños disfrutan esta clase. A veces es difícil, pero la maestra siempre les explica despacio. Ellos comprenden toda la información rápidamente. Los

The children count twenty ants!

But there are more... many more...

The children keep counting, one by one... **twenty-one**... **twenty- two**... **twenty-three**... **twenty- four**... **twenty-five**... **twenty- six**... **twenty-seven**... **twenty- eight**... **twenty-nine**... **thirty**.

But there are more... many more...

Thirty... **forty**... **fifty**... **sixty**... **seventy**... **eighty**... **ninety**... and a hundred!

There are a **hundred** ants!

Where do so many ants come from?

There are ants everywhere.

Children know that there are many ants inside an anthill. But the teacher tells them that it's time to go back to the classroom. It is time to continue with the other classes. Counting ants is fun, but the other classes are fun too. There is still much to learn.

School is a fun place. It is fun to learn about many things. The children are happy to learn so many things about the world.

Now it's math class. The children enjoy this class. Sometimes it is difficult, but the teacher always

| niños son muy inteligentes. Siempre resuelven todos los problemas fácilmente. | explains slowly. They understand all the information quickly. The children are very smart. They always solve all the problems easily. |

Acertijos (Riddles)

Ejercicio número uno (exercise number one):

Escribe el número según las palabras. (Write the number according to the words).

1. dos _____
2. dieciséis _____
3. cuarenta _____
4. cinco _____
5. veinte _____
6. once _____
7. treinta _____
8. cien _____
9. ocho _____
10. trece _____

Ejercicio número dos (exercise number two):

Combina las letras con el número correspondiente. (Match the word to the corresponding number).

uno ( )	5
dos ( )	10
tres ( )	15
cuatro ( )	6
cinco ( )	8
seis ( )	20
siete ( )	40
ocho ( )	100
nueve ( )	3

diez ( )	11
once ( )	2
doce ( )	19
trece ( )	1
catorce ( )	4
quince ( )	16
dieciséis ( )	18
diecisiete ( )	50
dieciocho ( )	13
diecinueve ( )	60
veinte ( )	7
treinta ( )	70
cuarenta ( )	9
cincuenta ( )	80
sesenta ( )	10
setenta ( )	12
ochenta ( )	30
noventa ( )	17
cien ( )	90

Ejercicio número tres (exercise number three):
Ordena los siguientes números del más pequeño al más grande. (Order the following numbers from the smallest to the largest).

1. seis	____
2. catorce	____
3. cincuenta	____
4. quince	____
5. siete	____
6. dieciséis	____
7. setenta	____
8. nueve	____
9. dieciocho	____

| 10. diez | ____ |

Soluciones (Solutions)

Ejercicio número uno (exercise number one):
Escribe el número según las palabras. (Write the number according to the words).

1. dos 2
2. dieciséis 16
3. cuarenta 40
4. cinco 5
5. veinte 20
6. once 11
7. treinta 30
8. cien 100
9. ocho 8
10. trece 13

Ejercicio número dos (exercise number two):
Combina las letras con el número correspondiente. (Match the word to the corresponding number).

Uno (1)	5
Dos (2)	14
Tres (3)	15
Cuatro (4)	6
Cinco (5)	8
Seis (6)	20
Siete (7)	40
Ocho (8)	100

Nueve (9)	3
Diez (10)	11
Once (11)	2
Doce (12)	19
Trece (13)	1
Catorce (14)	4
Quince (15)	16
Dieciséis (16)	18
Diecisiete (17)	50
Dieciocho (18)	13
Diecinueve (19)	60
Veinte (20)	7
Treinta (30)	70
Cuarenta (40)	9
Cincuenta (50)	80
Sesenta (60)	10
Setenta (70)	12
Ochenta (80)	30
Noventa (90)	17
Cien (100)	90

Ejercicio número tres (exercise number three):
Ordena los siguientes números del más pequeño al más grande. (Order the following numbers from the smallest to the largest).

1. seis
2. catorce
3. cincuenta
4. quince
5. siete
6. dieciséis
7. setenta
8. nueve
9. dieciocho
10. diez

seis
siete
nueve
diez
catorce
quince
dieciséis
dieciocho
cincuenta
setenta

Chapter 6
Capítulo Seis

Los Días de la Semana

Important words to remember:

Español	English	Pronunciation
lunes	Monday	/looh – nehs/
martes	Tuesday	/mahr – tehs/
miércoles	Wednesday	/mee – erh – koh – lehs/
jueves	Thursday	/hooh – eh – vehs/
viernes	Friday	/veeh – ehr – nehs/
sábado	Saturday	/sah – bah – doh/
domingo	Sunday	/doh – meehn – goh/

Los Días de la Semana (The Days of the Week)

Español	English
Marcela y Andrés son hermanos. Marcela tiene diez años y Andrés tiene nueve. Son muy unidos. Todo lo hacen juntos. Desde la mañana hasta la noche. Siempre están juntos. Tienen muchas actividades todos los días. Cada actividad la hacen juntos. Todo el tiempo hacen muchas actividades juntos. El día **lunes**, el primer día de la semana, ellos van a su clase de natación. Es la mejor manera de iniciar la semana. Ellos nadan dos	Marcela and Andrés are brothers. Marcela is ten years old and Andrés is nine. They are very united. They do everything together. From morning to night. They are always together. They have many activities every day. They do each activity together. They do lots of activities together all the time. On **Monday**, the first day of the week, they go to their swimming class. It is the best way to start the
horas después de clases. La natación es el deporte favorito de Andrés. Marcela también disfruta de la natación. Pero a ella le gusta	week. They swim for two hours after school. Swimming is Andrés's favorite sport. Marcela also enjoys swimming. But she

más otro deporte.

El **martes**, Marcela hace su actividad favorita... ¡bailar! Pero Andrés siempre va con ella.

Marcela necesita un compañero para bailar. Entonces, Andrés es su compañero preferido. Hay otros chicos en la clase de baile. Pero Marcela prefiere bailar con su hermano. Es el mejor del grupo.

Ahora los dos siempre bailan el martes después de clase.

Después de mucha actividad el lunes y martes, Marcela y Andrés descansan el **miércoles**.

Usualmente, van al centro comercial o al cine. Siempre van los dos. Siempre andan juntos. Siempre salen a todos lados. Esta semana, hay una nueva película de superhéroes en el cine. Marcela y Andrés llevan semanas esperando el estreno. Hoy es el día. La película está alucinante.

Los **jueves** están reservados para una actividad muy importante.

Este es el día que visitan a sus abuelitos. Después del colegio, salen rumbo a casa de sus abuelitos. Es un día muy especial porque la abuelita siempre tiene una comida sorpresa. Marcela y Andrés nunca saben qué delicia tiene preparada la abuelita.

Simplemente es una sorpresa genial. Esta semana, la sorpresa es torta de manzana. Marcela y Andrés quieren más y más... pero la abuelita les dice que guarden un

likes another sport more.

On **Tuesday**, Marcela does her favorite activity... dancing! But Andrés always goes with her.

Marcela needs a partner to dance. So, Andrés is his favorite partner. There are other boys in the dance class. But Marcela prefers to dance with her brother. He's the best of the bunch. Now the two of them always dance on Tuesday after class.

After a lot of activity on Monday and Tuesday, Marcela and Andrés take a break on **Wednesday**.

They usually go to the mall or the movies. The two of them always go. They always hang out together. They always come out everywhere. This week, there is a new superhero movie in theaters.

Marcela and Andrés have been waiting for the premiere for weeks. Today is the day. The movie is amazing.

Thursdays are reserved for very important activity. This is the day they visit their grandparents. After school, they go to their grandparents' house. It is a very special day because Grandma always has a surprise meal.

Marcela and Andrés never know what delicacy Grandma has prepared. It's just a cool surprise. This week, the surprise is apple pie. Marcela and Andrés want more and more... but the

poco para sus papás. El abuelito se pasa contando historias sobre el pasado. Los niños disfrutan las historias del abuelo.

    Los **viernes** son muy divertidos. Después del colegio, están libres para disfrutar su tiempo libre. Así que van a casa y terminan todas sus tareas. Así, ya no tienen tareas durante el fin de semana. Esta día, Marcela y Andrés se juntan con sus amigos del vecindario. Todos los chicos se reúnen para hablar sobre los acontecimientos de la semana. Marcela habla con las chicas mientras que Andrés juega con los chicos. Aunque están en grupos diferentes, nunca se separan.

    Siempre están cerca. Así son los hermanos tan unidos.

    El **sábado** es un día para jugar, hacer deporte, y ver un poco de televisión. Pero, la madre de Marcela y Andrés les pide que hagan los oficios de la casa. Entonces, los chicos deben limpiar su habitación, recoger la ropa sucia, y ordenar sus juguetes. No es divertido, pero es necesario.

    Después de terminar los oficios, están libres para jugar todo el día.

    El **domingo** es un día familiar. Usualmente, primos y tíos visitan

grandmother tells them to save some for their parents. Grandpa keeps telling stories about the past. Children enjoy grandfather stories.

    Fridays are so much fun. After school, they are free to enjoy their free time. So, they go home and finish all their homework. Thus, they no longer have tasks during the weekend. This day, Marcela and Andrés get together with their friends from the neighborhood. All the boys get together to talk about the events of the week. Marcela talks to the girls while Andrés plays with the boys. Although they are in different groups, they are never separated. They are always close. That's how close brothers are.

    Saturday is a day to play, do sports, and watch a little television. But Marcela and Andrés's mother asks them to do the housework. Then, the boys must clean their room, pick up the dirty clothes, and put their toys in order. It is not fun, but it is necessary. After finishing the trades, they are free to play all day.

    Sunday is a family day. Usually, cousins and uncles visit the house.

la casa. Toda la familia está unida para comer, o bien, ver la televisión. La familia de Marcela y Andrés es muy especial. Todos se quieren muchísimo.
 	
    Ahora conoces más acerca de estos dos chicos tan especiales.
    ¡Seguramente tú también eres una chica, o un chico, impresionante!
	The whole family is together to eat or watch television. Marcela and Andrés's family is very special. They all love each other very much.
	
	    Now you know more about these two very special guys. Surely you are also an awesome girl or boy!

Acertijos (Riddles)

Ejercicio número uno (exercise number one):
Escribe los días de la semana. (Write the days of the week).
1. _____
2. _____
3. _____
4. _____
5. _____
6. _____
7. _____

Ejercicio número dos (exercise number two):
    Encuentra los días de la semana en la sopa de letras. (Find de days of the week in the word search).

S	D	A	F	T	H	M	O	E	E	S
A	G	O	G	T	L	J	P	F	M	J
B	T	Ñ	M	X	Q	C	V	V	A	U
A	I	X	B	I	B	A	M	N	R	E
D	N	L	Ñ	K	N	D	F	B	T	V
O	N	G	F	E	Y	G	L	Ñ	E	E
H	J	A	B	B	Ñ	U	O	U	S	S
V	I	E	R	N	E	S	M	S	T	U
E	T	Y	H	B	N	S	T	F	G	A
L	K	L	U	N	E	S	U	O	I	O
M	I	E	R	C	O	L	E	S	M	N

Soluciones (Solutions)

Ejercicio número uno (exercise number one):
Escribe los días de la semana. (Write the days of the week).
1. lunes
2. martes
3. miércoles
4. jueves
5. viernes
6. sábado
7. domingo

Ejercicio número dos (exercise number two):

Encuentra los días de la semana en la sopa de letras. (Find de days of the week in the word search).

S	D	A	F	T	H	M	O	E	E	S
A	G	O	G	T	L	J	P	F	M	J
B	T	Ñ	M	X	Q	C	V	V	A	U
A	I	X	B	I	B	A	M	N	R	E
D	N	L	Ñ	K	N	D	F	B	T	V
O	N	G	F	E	Y	G	L	Ñ	E	E
H	J	A	B	B	Ñ	U	O	U	S	S
V	I	E	R	N	E	S	M	S	T	U
E	T	Y	H	B	N	S	T	F	G	A
L	K	L	U	N	E	S	U	O	I	O
M	I	E	R	C	O	L	E	S	M	N

Chapter 7
Capítulo Siete

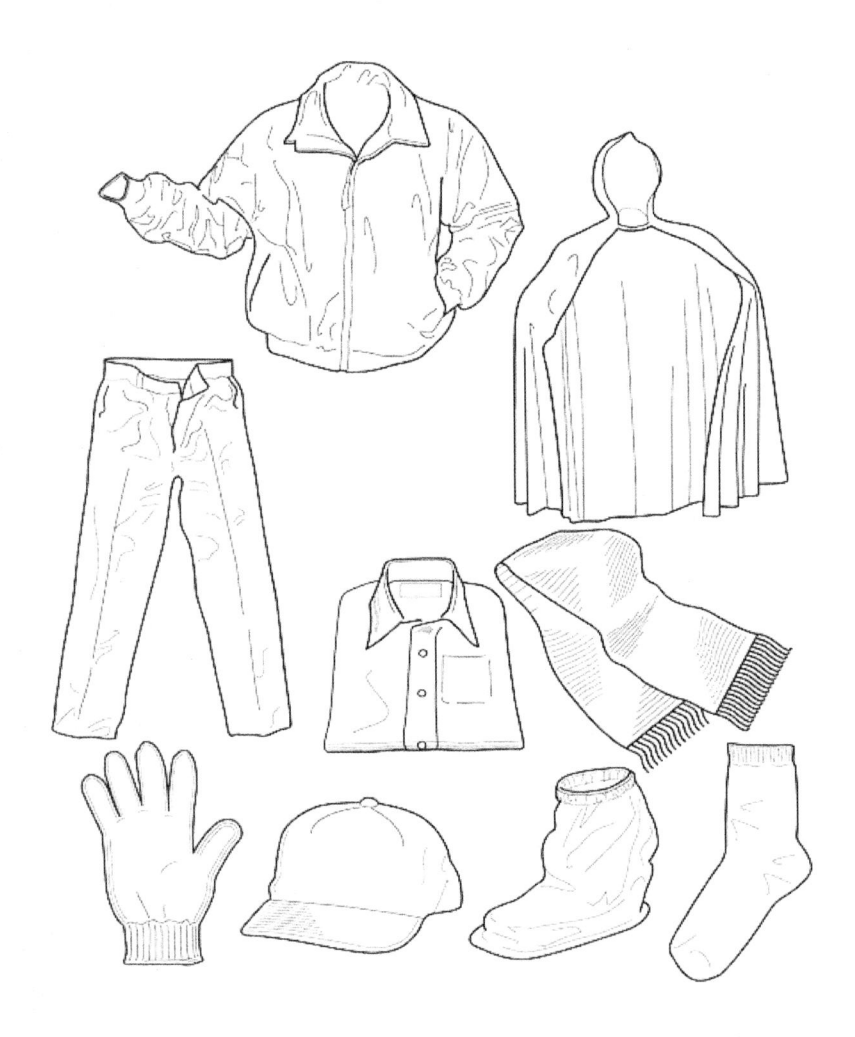

La Ropa

Important words to remember:

Español	English	Pronunciation
blusa	blouse	/blooh – sah/
camisa	shirt	/kah – mee – sah/
camiseta	shir	/kah – mee – seh - tah/
chaqueta	jacket	/chah – keh – tah/
medias	socks	/meh – deeh – ahs/
pantalón	trousers	/pahn – tah – lohn/
ropa interior	underwear	/roh – pah – eehn – teh – reeh –ohr/
suéter	sweater	/sooh – eh – tehr/
uniforme	uniform	/ooh – neeh – fohr – meh/
vaqueros	jeans	/vah – keh – rohs/
vestido	dress	/vehs – teeh – doh/
zapatillas	sneakers	/zah – pah – teeh – yahs/
zapatos	shoes	/zah – pah – tohs/

La Ropa (The Clothes)

Español	English
Marcela y Andrés necesitan ropa nueva. Su ropa ya está muy vieja y gastada. Por eso, sus padres los llevarán el fin de semana a comprar ropa nueva. Marcela está muy emocionada ya que quiere un **vestido** nuevo. Andrés está feliz	Marcela and Andrés need new clothes. His clothes are already very old and worn. So, their parents will take them shopping for new clothes at the weekend. Marcela is very excited as she wants a new **dress**. Andrés is happy because he wants

porque quiere unos **vaqueros** nuevos. Los dos chicos tienen en mente qué ropa quieren.

La familia va al centro comercial el domingo por la mañana. En el centro comercial, hay muchas tiendas. Hay una gran variedad de artículos para escoger. Marcela y Andrés no saben por dónde empezar... hay tanto de dónde escoger.

Primero, van a una tienda de ropa deportiva. Los chicos necesitan **zapatillas** nuevas para hacer ejercicio. Marcela ve unas zapatillas rosadas mientras Andrés ve unas rojas. El padre de ambos les dice que no. Ellos deben buscar unas zapatillas adecuadas para el entrenamiento y no por el color.

Entonces, compran unas zapatillas diseñadas para correr y saltar.

Luego, van a una tienda con muchos abrigos, **suéteres**, y **chaquetas**. Pronto vendrá el clima frío. Es por ello que los chicos deben tener ropa adecuada para este clima. A los chicos no les gusta escoger este tipo de ropa... es muy aburrido. ¡Es mejor escoger **camisetas** y **zapatos**!

Ahora, los chicos necesitan ropa para el colegio. En el colegio, usan **uniforme**. Pero, su madre les dice que necesitan **medias** y **ropa interior**. Qué aburrido... se pasan una hora escogiendo la ropa adecuada. Los chicos ya están

new **jeans**. The two kids have in mind what clothes they want.

The family goes to the mall on Sunday morning. In the mall, there are many stores. There are a wide variety of items to choose from. Marcela and Andrés don't know where to start... there is so much to choose from.

First, they go to a sportswear store. The kids need new shoes to exercise. Marcela sees pink **sneakers** while Andrés sees red ones. Their father says no. They should look for suitable shoes for training and not for color. So, they buy shoes designed for running and jumping.

Then they go to a store with lots of coats, **sweaters**, and **jackets**.

Cold weather will come soon. That is why boys should have appropriate clothing for this climate. The kids do not like to choose this type of clothing ... it is very boring. It is better to choose **shirts** and **shoes**!

Now, the kids need clothes for school. At school, they wear a **uniform**. But their mother tells them that they need **socks** and **underwear**. How boring ... they spend an hour choosing the right clothes. The kids are already tired of

cansados de ver ropa aburrida.

La hora del almuerzo está aquí. La familia va a un restaurante de pizza. Los chicos se emocionan ya que comerán pizza. Andrés adora la pizza. Pero la comida favorita de Marcela es la pasta. A ella le encanta el espagueti. Todos comen su comida preferida. Es un almuerzo delicioso.

Después del almuerzo, la familia continúa buscando más ropa.
Andrés está desesperado por ver una camiseta nueva. Hay muchos diseños de superhéroes. Él quiere una de Batman. Andrés no quiere una **camisa** o **pantalón** formal.

Marcela está emocionada por un vestido rosa. Es largo y tiene muchas decoraciones lindas. Tiene una decoración de princesa.
Realmente parece una princesa salida de un cuento de hadas. También le gusta una **blusa** de muchos colores.

Al final, los chicos tienen lo que quieren. Andrés tiene la camiseta de superhéroes y unos vaqueros nuevos. Los vaqueros son azules.

looking at boring clothes.

Lunchtime is here. The family goes to a pizza restaurant. The children are excited as they will eat pizza.
Andrés loves pizza. But Marcela's favorite food is pasta. She loves spaghetti. Everyone eats their favorite food. It's a delicious lunch.

After lunch, the family continues to search for more clothes. Andrés is desperate to see a new shirt.
There are many superhero designs. He wants one from Batman. Andrés does not want a formal **shirt** or a pair of **trousers**.

Marcela is excited about a pink dress. It is long and has many cute decorations. It has princess decoration. She looks like a princess out of a fairy tale. She also likes a very colorful **blouse**.

In the end, the children have what they want. Andrés has a superhero

Están de moda. Los amigos de Andrés estarán impresionados con su nueva ropa.

Marcela no obtuvo el vestido de princesa. Al final, ella tiene algo mejor. Tiene un vestido largo y rosa. Parece como si fuera sirena. Además, tiene otro vestido. Es amarillo y parece un girasol. Ella está encantada con sus nuevos vestidos. Están de lo mejor.

Ahora, los dos chicos están felices. Después de un día largo de compras, la familia va a casa. Es hora de descansar. Mañana deben ir a colegio. Van a estrenar su nueva ropa para el colegio.

Tristemente, deben esperar hasta el próximo fin de semana para estrenar su ropa nueva.

shirt and new jeans. The jeans are blue. Are trendy. Andrés's friends will be impressed with his new clothes.

Marcela did not get the princess's dress. In the end, she has something better. She has a long pink dress. She looks like a mermaid. Also, she has another dress. It is yellow and looks like a sunflower. She is delighted with her new dresses. They are the best.

Now, the two boys are happy. After a long day of shopping, the family goes home. It's time to rest. Tomorrow they must go to school. They are going to release their new clothes for school. Sadly, they must wait until next weekend to show off their new clothes.

Acertijos (Riddles)

Ejercicio número uno (exercise number one):

Coloca las letras en el orden correcto. (Place the letters in the correct order).
1. treseu _____
2. qaveusor _____
3. tsoazap _____
4. doitsve ___ _____

5. estamica _____

Ejercicio número dos (exercise number two):

Escribe la palabra correspondiente a la imagen. (Write the corresponding word for the image).

1. _____

2. _____

3. _____

4. _____

5. _____

Ejercicio número tres (exercise number three):
Combina la palabra en español con la palabra en inglés. (Match the Spanish with theEnglish word).

Suéter	Blouse
camiseta	shirt
uniforme	t-shirt
chaqueta	jacket
vaqueros	socks
ropa interior	underwear
camisa	sweater
zapatillas	uniform
medias	jeans
blusa	dress
zapatos	sneakers
vestido	shoes

Soluciones (Solutions)

Ejercicio número uno (exercise number one):
Coloca las letras en el orden correcto. (Place the letters in the correct order).
1. treseu **suéter**
2. qaveusor **vaqueros**
3. tsoazap **zapatos**

4. doitsve **vestido**

5. estamica **camiseta**

Ejercicio número dos (exercise number two):

Escribe la palabra correspondiente a la imagen. (Write the corresponding word for the image).

1. zapatos

2. vestido

3. camiseta

4. medias

5. suéter

Ejercicio número tres (exercise number three):

Combina la palabra en español con la palabra en inglés. (Match the Spanish with the English word).

suéter	**sweater**
camiseta	**t-shirt**
uniforme	**uniform**
chaqueta	**jacket**
vaqueros	**jeans**
ropa interior	**underwear**
camisa	**shirt**
zapatillas	**sneakers**
medias	**socks**
blusa	**blouse**
zapatos	**shoes**
vestido	**dress**

Chapter 8
Capítulo Ocho

La Escuela

Important words to remember:

Español	English	Pronunciation
arte	art	/ahr – teh/
ciencias naturales	natural sciences	/seeh -ehn – seeh – ahs - nah – too – rah – lehs/
clase	class	/klah – seh/
divisiones	divisions	/deeh – veeh – seeh - oh –nehs/
educación física	physical education	/eh – dooh – kah – seeh –ohn – feeh – seeh – kah/
escuela	school	/ehs – kooh – eh – lah/
estudios sociales	social studies	/ehs – tooh – deeh – ohs– soh – seeh – ah – lehs/
examen	exam	/ehk – sah – mehn/
grado	grade	/grah – doh/
idiomas	languages	/eeh – deeh – oh – mahs/
lectura	reading	/lehk – tooh – rah/
lenguaje	language arts	/lehn – gooh – ah – heh/
maestra	teacher	/mah – ehs – trah/
matemáticas	mathematics	/mah – teh – mah – teeh– kahs/

materias	subjects	/mah – teh – reeh – ahs/
multiplicaciones	multiplications	/moohl – teeh – pleeh –kah – seeh – ohn/
primaria	primary	/preeh – mah -reeh – ah/
restas	subtraction	/rehs – tahs/
sumas	sums	/sooh – mahs/

La Escuela (School)

Español	English
Amanda y Olivia son las mejores amigas del mundo. Ellas son vecinas. Viven en el mismo vecindario. De hecho, viven en la misma calle. Para ser específicos, viven a la par. Sus papás también son amigos. Tienen muchos años de conocerse. Amanda y Olivia van a la misma **escuela**. Las chicas están en el mismo grado y tienen la misma **maestra**. Tienen nueve años. Están en el tercer año de **primaria**. Ambas son chicas muy inteligentes. Son las mejores estudiantes de su **grado**. La clase preferida de Amanda es matemáticas. A ella le encanta estudiar números. Ella siempre pone mucha atención en la clase de **matemáticas**. Le encanta hacer **sumas**, **restas**, **multiplicaciones** y	Amanda and Olivia are the best friends in the world. They are neighbors. They live in the same neighborhood. In fact, they live on the same street. To be specific, they live next door. Their parents are friends too. They have known each other for many years. Amanda and Olivia go to the same **school**. The girls are in the same grade and have the same **teacher**. They are nine years old. They are in the third year of **primary** school. They are both very smart girls. They are the best students in their **grade**. Amanda's favorite class is math. She loves studying numbers. She always pays a lot of attention in **math** class. She loves to do

divisiones. No importa si la maestra deja muchos ejercicios. Amanda siempre los hacen felizmente.

Olivia no le gusta la matemática tanto como a Amanda. Para Olivia, su clase preferida es **lenguaje**. A ella le encanta aprender sobre idiomas. Los **idiomas** son tan interesantes para ella. Le gusta aprender palabras nuevas.

También le encanta escribir historias sobre sus personajes favoritos.

Además de matemáticas y lenguaje, las niñas estudian **ciencias naturales, estudios sociales, arte, educación física**, y **lectura**. A ambas les gusta leer mucho. En su casa tienen muchos libros sobre distintos temas.

Siempre hay algo nuevo que leer en casa de Amanda. Los padres de Olivia le compran historietas todo el tiempo.

Olivia lee sus historietas en lugar de ver televisión.

Todos los chicos admiran a estas dos niñas. Ellas son las más estudiosas y diligentes. Siempre hacen sus tareas.

Siempre participan en la **clase**, y siempre son puntuales. La maestra las considera como sus mejores alumnas.

---

addition, subtraction, multiplication, and **division**. It doesn't matter if the teacher leaves a lot of exercise. Amanda always makes them happy.

Olivia doesn't like math as much as Amanda. For Olivia, her favorite class is **language**. She loves learning about **languages**. Languages are so interesting to her. Likes to learn new words. She also loves to write stories about her favorite characters.

In addition to **math** and **language arts**, girls study **science, social studies, art, physical education**, and **reading**. They both like to read a lot. They have many books at home on different subjects. There is always something new to read at Amanda's house.

Olivia's parents buy her comics all the time. Olivia reads her comics instead of watching television.

All the kids look up to these two girls. They are the most studious and diligent. They always do their homework. They always participate in **class**, and they are always punctual. The teacher considers them her best

Las chicas tienen un **examen**	
de matemáticas hoy. Amanda está preparada. Se siente muy segura de sí misma. Olivia también está preparada, pero está un poco nerviosa. Amanda le asegura que todo estará bien. Le dice que ella es inteligente.

Seguramente Amanda hará un buen examen. No tiene razón para estar nerviosa.

La próxima semana hay un examen de lenguaje. Olivia está emocionada porque sabe todo el contenido para ese examen. No hay duda de que hará un buen examen.

Entonces, Olivia ayuda a Amanda a estudiar para el examen. Amanda y Olivia pasan una hora después de clases estudiando para el examen de lenguaje. Luego, Amanda se va para su casa. Las chicas continúan estudiando hasta la hora de cena. Las chicas repasan ciencias naturales y estudios sociales.

Hay mucho que leer en esas dos **materias**. Los temas son interesantes.

Pero si piensas que las chicas solamente estudian, estás equivocado. Las chicas también les gusta mucho hacer deporte. Juegan en el equipo de fútbol de su escuela. Y,

¡sorpresa! También son | students.

The girls have a math **test** today. Amanda is ready. She feels very sure of herself.

Olivia is ready too, but she's a little nervous. Amanda assures her that everything will be fine. It tells her that she is smart. Amanda will surely do a good test. She has no reason to be nervous.

Next week there is a language test. Olivia is excited because she knows all the content for that exam. There is no doubt that she will do a good test. So, Olivia helps Amanda study for the test. Amanda and Olivia spend an hour after school studying for the language test. Then Amanda goes home. The girls continue studying until dinner time. The girls review science and social studies. There is a lot to read in those two **subjects**. The topics are interesting.

But if you think that girls only study, you are wrong. Girls also really like to play sports. They play on their school's soccer team. And surprise! They are also the best players on their team. |

las mejores jugadoras de su equipo. Amanda es la goleadora mientras que Olivia	Amanda is the scorer while
es la arquera. Entre las dos, anotan muchos goles y detienen los goles de los demás equipos. Son una combinación invencible.	Olivia is the goalkeeper. Between the two, they score many goals and stop the other teams' goals. They are an invincible combination.

Acertijos (Riddles)

Ejercicio número uno (exercise number one):
Marca la palabra que no corresponde en la serie. (Mark the word that does not belong in the series).

1. matemáticas ciencias correr estudios sociales lenguaje
2. estudiante maestra escuela video profesor
3. clase examen lectura estudiar jugar
4. inteligente diligente feliz nerviosa preparada
5. viajar grado clase compañero maestra

Ejercicio número dos (exercise number two):
Escribe la palabra correcta en inglés para el siguiente vocabulario. (Write the correct English word for the following vocabulary).

1. estudiante _____
2. maestra _____
3. clase _____
4. materia _____
5. examen _____
6. compañero _____
7. matemáticas _____

8. lectura _____

9. idioma _____

10. inteligente _____

Soluciones (Solutions)

Ejercicio número uno (exercise number one):
Marca la palabra que no corresponde en la serie. (Mark the word that does not belong in the series).
1. matemáticas ciencias **correr** estudios sociales lenguaje
2. estudiante maestra escuela **video** profesor
3. clase examen lectura estudiar **jugar**
4. inteligente diligente feliz **nerviosa** preparada
5. **viajar** grado clase compañero maestra

Ejercicio número dos (exercise number two):
Escribe la palabra correcta en inglés para el siguiente vocabulario. (Write the correct English word for the following vocabulary).

1. estudiante **student**

2. maestra **teacher**

3. clase **class**

4. materia **subject**

5. examen **test**

6. compañero **classmate**

7. matemáticas **mathematics**

8. lectura **reading**

9. idioma **language**

10. inteligente **intelligent**

Chapter 9
Capítulo Nueve

La Familia

Important words to remember:

Español	English	Pronunciation
abuela	grandmother	/abooh – eh – lah/
abuelo	grandfather	/abooh – eh – loh/
esposa	wife	/ehs – poh – sah/
esposo	husband	/ehs – poh – soh/
familia	family	/fah – meeh – leeh – ah/
hermana	sister	/ehr – mah - nah/
hermano	brother	/ehr – mah - noh/
hija	daughter	/eeh – hah/
hijo	son	/eeh – hoh/
madre	mother	/mah – dreh/
nieta	granddaughter	/neeh – eh – tah/
nieto	grandson	/neeh – eh – toh/
padre	father	/pah – dreh/
primos	cousins	/preeh – mohs/
tía	aunt	/teeh – ah/
tío	uncle	/teeh – oh/

La Familia (The Family)

Español	English
Fernando es un niño muy inquieto y activo. Le gusta hacer todo tipo de actividades. A él le encanta jugar en casa con sus hermanos. Su **hermana** mayor, Blanca, tiene diez años. Su **hermano** menor, Diego, tiene siete años. Fernando tiene ocho años. Los tres hermanos juegan todo el tiempo. Se pasan su tiempo libre con toda clase de actividades divertidas. El **padre** de los chicos es don Miguel. Él es contador. Trabaja en una empresa que fabrica alimentos. Tiene un trabajo de tiempo completo. Sale de la casa a las seis de la mañana y regresa a las seis de la tarde. Él es serio y estricto pero muy cariñoso con sus hijos. Siempre está dispuesto a jugar con ellos aun cuando está cansado. La **madre** de los hermanos es doña Raquel. Ella es muy hogareña. Siempre le gusta cocinar y preparar deliciosas meriendas. Pero las meriendas son saludables. A ella no le gusta mucha azúcar en la comida de sus niños. Lo importante es la salud. Los niños saben que siempre tienen comida muy saludable con su madre. La **familia** es muy unida.	Fernando is a very restless and active child. He likes to do all kinds of activities. He loves to play at home with his brothers. His older **sister**, Blanca, is ten years old. His younger **brother**, Diego, is seven years old. Fernando is eight years old. The three brothers play all the time. They spend their free time with all kinds of fun activities. The kids' **father** is Don Miguel. He is an accountant. He works in a company that manufactures food. He has a full-time job. He leaves the house at six in the morning and returns at six in the afternoon. He is serious and strict but very affectionate with his children. He is always willing to play with them even when he is tired. Doña Raquel is the siblings' **mother**. She is very homey. She always likes to cook and prepare delicious snacks. But the snacks are healthy. She doesn't like a lot of sugar in her children's food. The important thing is health. Children know that they always have very healthy food with their mother. The **family** is very close. They are always together all the time. They

Siempre están juntos todo el tiempo. Hacen tiempo para estar	make time to be together at dinner
juntos en la hora de la cena. También hacen muchas actividades divertidas en familia. Este fin de semana, irán a un campamento. En este campamento estará al aire libre todo el fin de semana. Es algo muy divertido ya que ellos viven en una ciudad muy grande. Por eso, necesitan estar un tiempo fuera del ruido de la ciudad. Los niños están felices de pasar el fin de semana en el campo. Pero no estarán ellos solos. También llegarán sus **tíos**, **tías**, y primos. Sus abuelitos también estarán ahí. El **abuelo** Jorge es muy activo. A él le encanta estar en actividades al aire libre. Ya tiene muchos años de edad, pero igual le gusta jugar al basquetbol. La **abuela** María es muy divertida. A ella le encanta leer mientras respira aire fresco. Los chicos tienen nueve primos. Cuando todos los **primos** se juntan, se hace una buena fiesta. Los chicos juegan al fútbol mientras las chicas corren por todo el campo. Se	time. They also do lots of fun family activities. This weekend, they are going to camp. In this camp, you will be outdoors all weekend. It's a lot of fun since they live in a very big city. Therefore, they need to be away from the noise of the city for a while. The children are happy to spend the weekend in the country. But they will not be alone. Their **uncles**, **aunts**, and cousins will also arrive. Their grandparents will be there too. **Grandpa** Jorge is very active. He loves being in outdoor activities. He's very old now, but he still likes to play basketball. **Grandma** Maria is very funny. She loves to read while breathing fresh air. The boys have nine cousins. When all the **cousins** get together, it makes a good party. The boys play soccer while the girls run across the field. They have a lot of fun playing with all the cousins. It is a big and loving family. In this camp, there is also a special occasion to celebrate. It's Grandpa Jorge's birthday. Grandfather Jorge is

divierten mucho jugando entre todos los primos. Es una familia grande y amorosa.

En este campamento, también hay una ocasión especial para celebrar. Es el cumpleaños del abuelo Jorge. El abuelo Jorge cumple setenta y cinco años. Es una celebración muy especial. Toda la familia lo adora. Miguel y su **esposa** Raquel tienen una sorpresa muy especial. La abuela María también tiene una sorpresa genial.

¿Cuál es la sorpresa?

Toda la familia ha preparado un pastel muy singular. El pastel es de chocolate y vainilla. Pero en el centro tiene una fotografía de toda la familia. Está el **esposo**, **hijos** e **hijas**, **nietos** y **nietas** del abuelo Jorge. Cuando lo ve, el abuelo llora de la emoción. Sin duda, este es el mejor cumpleaños del abuelo Jorge. Él es muy feliz de tener una familia tan grande.

El abuelo dice, ¡mi familia es la mejor del mundo!

75 years old. It is a very special celebration. The whole family loves it. Miguel and his **wife** Raquel have a very special surprise. Grandma Maria has a great surprise too.

What is the surprise?

The whole family has prepared a very unique cake. The cake is chocolate and vanilla. But in the center, it has a photograph of the whole family. There is the **husband**, **sons** and **daughters**, **grandsons** and **granddaughters** of Grandfather Jorge. When he sees it, Grandpa cries with feeling.

Without a doubt, this is Grandpa Jorge's best birthday. He is very happy to have such a big family. Grandpa says my family is the best in the world!

Acertijos (Riddles)

Ejercicio número uno (exercise number one):

Escoge la palabra correcta para completer la frase. (Choose the correct word to complete the phrase).

1. Mi_____cocina comida muy deliciosa. (abuela / mascota / maestra)
2. Mis_____juegan fútbol conmigo en el campo. (clases / primos / libros)
3. Tengo tres _____. (inteligente / nuevo / hermanos)
4. Mi_____trabaja como doctora. (madre / gato / televisión)
5. La_____Pamela tiene 25 años. (tía / tío / tíos)

Ejercicio número dos (exercise number two):

Encuentra las siguientes palabras dentro de la sopa de letras. (Find the following words in the word search).

tía abuelo nieto hija padre hermano primos esposa

A	W	S	T	G	C	X	H	I	J	A
B	E	R	N	M	X	S	S	B	N	Q
U	X	V	D	C	R	I	M	V	B	P
E	C	Z	A	T	I	A	Q	W	K	A
L	G	H	H	N	Y	G	F	Ñ	L	D
O	Z	N	I	E	T	O	Y	C	N	R
Q	W	C	B	G	R	J	Ñ	V	X	E
L	I	B	U	U	O	M	H	M	S	Z
E	S	P	O	S	A	P	A	K	W	Y
K	P	R	I	M	O	S	W	N	O	Ñ
K	T	R	T	U	I	P	R	G	O	A

Ejercicio número tres (exercise number three):

Selecciona la opción correct. (Select the correct option).

77

1. El hermano de mi padre es mi_____.
   a. Tío
   b. Tía
   c. Primo
2. La madre de mi madre es mi_____.
   a. Hermana
   b. Abuela
   c. Prima
3. Los hijos de mi tía son mis_____.
   a. Hermanos
   b. Primos
   c. Abuelos

Soluciones (Solutions)

Ejercicio número uno (exercise number one):
Escoge la palabra correcta para completer la frase. (Choose the correct word to complete the phrase).

1. Mi_____cocina comida muy deliciosa. (**abuela** / mascota / maestra)

2. Mis_____juegan fútbol conmigo en el campo. (clases / **primos** / libros)

3. Tengo tres_____ (inteligente / nuevo / **hermanos**)

4. Mi_____trabaja como doctora. (**madre** / gato / televisión)

5. La_____Pamela tiene 25 años. (**tía** / tío / tíos)

Ejercicio número dos (exercise number two):
Encuentra las siguientes palabras dentro de la sopa de letras. (Find the following words in the word search).

tía abuelo nieto hija padre hermano primos esposa

A	W	S	T	G	C	X	H	I	J	A
B	E	R	N	M	X	S	S	B	N	Q
U	X	V	D	C	R	I	M	V	B	P
E	C	Z	A	T	I	A	Q	W	K	A
L	G	H	H	N	Y	G	F	Ñ	L	D
O	Z	N	I	E	T	O	Y	C	N	R
Q	W	C	B	G	R	J	Ñ	V	X	E
L	I	B	U	U	O	M	H	M	S	Z
E	S	P	O	S	A	P	A	K	W	Y
K	P	R	I	M	O	S	W	N	O	Ñ
K	T	R	T	U	I	P	R	G	O	A

Ejercicio número tres (exercise number three):
Selecciona la opción correct. (Select the correct option).

1. El hermano de mi padre es mi_____.
   a. Tío
   b. Tía
   c. Primo
2. La madre de mi madre es mi_____.
   a. Hermana
   b. Abuela
   c. Prima
3. Los hijos de mi tía son mis_____.
   a. Hermanos
   b. Primos
   c. Abuelos

Chapter 10
Capítulo Diez

Los Juego

Important words to remember:

Español	English	Pronunciation
adivinanzas	riddles	/ah – deeh – veeh – nahn – zahs/
ajedrez	chess	/ah – heh – drehs/
balón	ball	/bah – lohn/
basquetbol	basketball	/bahs – keht – bol/
béisbol	baseball	/beh – eehs – bohl/
cancha	court	/kahn – chah/
congelados	freeze tag	/kohn – heh – lah – dohs/
damas	ladies	/dah – mahs/
damas chinas	Chinese checkers	/ dah – mahs cheeh – nahs/
deportes	sports	/deh – pohr – tehs/
escondite	hiding place	/ehs – kohn – deeh – teh/
fútbol	soccer	/fooht – bohl/
juegos de mesa	table games	/hooh – eh – gohs – deh meh - sah/
juegos de palabras	word games	/hooh – eh – gohs – deh pah – lah – brahs/
rimas	rhymes	/reeh – mahs/
tablero	board	/tah – bleh – roh/

tenta	tag	/tehn – tah/
trabalenguas	tongue twister	/trah – bah – looh – ehn – gooh – ahs/
video juegos	video game	/veeh – deeh – oh – hooh – eh –gohs/
volibol	volleyball	/voh – leeh – bohl/

Los Juegos (The Games)

Español	English
¿Te gustan los juegos?	Do you like games?
Hay muchos juegos que pueden jugar cuando quieras. Por ejemplo, hay juegos de mesa. Los **juegos de mesa** son muy divertidos. Lo mejor es que no necesitas equipo especial para jugarlos. Únicamente necesitas un espacio libre para poner el **tablero,** y ¡listo!	There are many games that you can play whenever you want. For example, there are board games. **Board games** are great fun. The best part is that you don't need special equipment to play them. You only need a free space to put the **board**, and voila!
Los juegos de mesa usualmente son para dos o más jugares. Hay juegos como las **damas**, el **ajedrez**, y las **damas chinas**. También hay otros juegos como los dominó y las cartas. Estos son juegos que puedes jugar por horas. Son ideales para un día lluvioso porque no puedes salir a jugar afuera.	Board games are usually for two or more players. There are games like checkers, chess, and Chinese checkers. There are also other games like dominoes and cards.
Cuando el día es soleado, hay	These are games that you can play for hours. They are ideal for a rainy day because you can't go outside to play.

muchos juegos que puedes jugar con tus amigos. Juegos como **tenta**, **congelados**, o al **escondite**. Necesitas mucha energía ya que estarás corriendo todo el tiempo. Debes tomar mucha agua también la realizar estas actividades. Estos juegos son perfectos para jugar en el patio de tu escuela con todos tus amigos.

Seguramente se divertirán muchísimo.

También puedes hacer deportes con tus amigos. **Deportes** como el **fútbol** son muy fáciles de jugar.

Solamente necesitas un balón para jugar. No necesitas más equipo.

Con tus amigos, puedéis jugar por horas al aire libre.

Pero el fútbol no es el único deporte que puedes jugar. También existen otros deportes como el **basquetbol**, **béisbol**, y el **volibol**. Cualquiera de estos deportes es una excelente manera de jugar en equipo con todos tus amigos.

Para jugar al basquetbol, necesitas un aro además del **balón**.

Usualmente puedes encontrar una **cancha** de basquetbol en el parque de tu vecindario. Si te gusta el volibol, seguramente hay una cancha en el parque también.

Necesitas un balón diferente para jugar volibol. Pero eso no es problema.

When the day is sunny, there are many games that you can play with your friends. Games like tag, freeze tag or hide and seek. You need a lot of energy since you will be running all the time. You should also drink a lot of water when doing these activities. These games are perfect to play in your schoolyard with all your friends. They will surely have a lot of fun.

You can also do sports with your friends. Sports like soccer are very easy to play. You only need one ball to play. You don't need more equipment. With your friends, you can play for hours outside.

But soccer is not the only sport you can play. There are also other sports such as basketball, baseball, and volleyball. Any of these sports is a great way to play as a team with all your friends.

To play basketball, you need a hoop in addition to the ball. You can usually find a basketball court in your neighborhood park. If you like volleyball, surely there is a court in the park too. You need a different ball to play volleyball.

But that is not a

problem. Do you know

something?

There are many, many games.

¿Sabes una cosa?

Hay muchos, muchos juegos.

Hay **juegos de palabras**. Por ejemplo, las **rimas** y las **adivinanzas** son muy divertidas. A veces son difíciles de acertar.

¡Pero ese es el chiste! La idea es pasar un buen tiempo tratando de adivinar la respuesta. Los **trabalenguas** también son muy chistosos. Es un poco difícil decirles, pero con bastante práctica lo lograrás.

También existen los **videojuegos**. Estos se juegan en una computadora o una consola de juegos. Existe una variedad de juegos. Algunos son muy fáciles de aprender. Otros requieren mucha práctica. Lo mejor es que puedes jugar con todos tus amigos. Con una conexión a internet, puedes jugar con todos tus amigos en línea. Si no puedes salir de casa, jugar en línea puede ser de lo más divertido.

Realmente no importa qué juego te divierte más. Lo importante es jugar con tu familia y tus amigos. La vida siempre es mejor con juegos divertidos. Ahora conoces todos los diferentes tipos de juegos. Puedes escoger los que más te gustan. Puedes divertirte con tus amigos en la escuela o en casa.

Puedes reunir a todos tus amigos en un videojuego en línea.

Después, puedes salir al aire libre a

There are word games. For example, rhymes and riddles are a lot of fun. Sometimes they are difficult to hit. But that's the joke! The idea is to spend a good time trying to guess the answer. The tongue twisters are also very funny. It's a bit difficult to tell them, but with enough practice, you will succeed.

There are also video games. These are played on a computer or a game console. There are a variety of games. Some are very easy to learn. Others take a lot of practice. The best thing is that you can play with all your friends. With an internet connection, you can play with all your friends online. If you can't leave the house, playing online can be a lot of fun.

It doesn't matter which game you enjoy the most. The important thing is to play with your family and friends. Life is always better with fun games. Now you know all the different types of games. You can choose the ones you like the most. You can have fun with your friends at school or home. You can gather all your friends in an online video game. Afterward, you can go outside to practice your favorite sport.

practicar tu deporte favorito. ¡Solamente debes utilizar tu imaginación y creatividad!	You just have to use your imagination and creativity!

Acertijos (Riddles)

Ejercicio número uno (exercise number one):
Responde las preguntas. (Answer the questions).
1. Escribe los nombres de tres juegos:
   a. _____
   b. _____
   c. _____
2. Escribe los nombres de tres deportes:
   a. _____
   b. _____
   c. _____
3. Escribe el nombre de tu juego favorito: _____
4. Escribe el nombre de tu deporte favorito: _____

Ejercicio número dos (exercise number two):
Coloca las letras en el orden correcto. (Place the letters in the correct order).
1. obvlilo _____
2. mair _
3. sdaam _____
4. zjarede _____
5. dtienecso _____

Ejercicio número tres (exercise number three):

Escribe el nombre del juego o deporte. (Write the name of the game or sport).

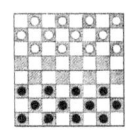

_____   _____   _____   _____   _____

Soluciones (Solutions)

Ejercicio número uno (exercise number one):
Responde las preguntas. (Answer the questions). - EXAMPLES -
1. Escribe los nombres de tres juegos:
   a. ajedrez
   b. damas
   c. dominó

2. Escribe los nombres de tres deportes:
   a. volibol
   b. fútbol
   c. basquetbol

3. Escribe el nombre de tu juego favorito:
   Damas chinas

4. Escribe el nombre de tu deporte favorito:
   Béisbol

Ejercicio número dos (exercise number two):
Coloca las letras en el orden correcto. (Place the letters in the correct order).
1. obvlilo **volibol**
2. mair **rima**
3. sdaam **damas**

4. zjarede **ajedrez**
5. dtienecso **escondite**

Ejercicio número tres (exercise number three):
Escribe el nombre del juego o deporte. (Write the name of the game or sport).

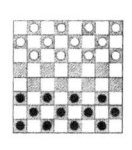

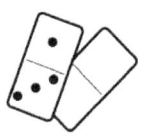

damas   domino   videojuego   fútbol   escondite

Chapter 11
Capítulo Once

Me Gusta Ir a la Escuela

Important words to remember

Español	English	Pronunciation
ciudad	city	/seeh – ooh – dahd/
amigos	friends	/ah – meeh – gohs/
tardes	afternoon	/tahr – dehs/
pasteles	cakes	/pahs – teh – lehs/
divertido	fun	/deeh – vehr – teeh – doh/
trabajo	job	/trah – bah – hoh/
primaria	primary	/preeh – mah – reeh – ah/
vecindario	neighborhood	/veh – seehn – dah – reeh – oh/
juntos	together	/hoohn – tohs/
maestra	teacher	/mah – ehs – trah/
estudiando	studying	/ehs – tooh – deeh – ahn – doh/
palabras	word	/pah – lah – brahs/
computadoras	computers	/kohm – pooh – tah – doh – rahs/
creativo	creative	/kreh – ah – teeh – voh/
proyectos	projects	/proh – yehk – tohs/
exámenes	exams	/ehk – sah – meh – nehs/

nervioso	nervous	/nehr – veeh – oh – soh/
preocupado	worried	/preh – oh – kooh – pah – doh/
estudiante	student	/ehs – tooh – deeh – ahn – teh/
astronauta	astronaut	/ahs – troh – nawh – tah/
inteligente	intelligent	/eehn – teh – leeh – hehn – teh/
talentosa	talented	/tah – lehn – toh – sah/
aprender	learning	/ah – prehn – dehr/
espacio	space	/ehs – pah – seeh – oh/
planetas	planets	/plah – neh – tahs
extraterrestres	extraterrestrials	/ehks – trah – teh – rehs – trehs/

Me Gusta Ir a la Escuela (I Like Going to School)

Español	English
Hola, me llamo José. Pero todos mis amigos me dicen Pepe. Tengo diez años. Vivo en una **ciudad** muy grande. Vivo en una casa dentro de un vecindario muy divertido. Tengo muchos **amigos** en mi vecindario. Todos los días, salimos a la calle a jugar fútbol. Es muy alegre. Tenemos partidos emocionantes todas las **tardes**. Tengo una familia muy grande. Mi madre se llama Julieta. Ella es muy amorosa. Hace los mejores **pasteles** del mundo. Es la mejor mamá del mundo. Mi padre se	Hello, my name is Jose. But all my friends call me Pepe. I am ten years old. I live in a very big **city**. I live in a house in a very fun neighborhood. I have many **friends** in my neighborhood. Every day, we go outside to play soccer. It is very fund. We have exciting games every **afternoon**. I have a very large family. My mother is called Julieta. She is very loving. She makes the best **cakes** in the world. She is the best

llama Francisco. Es muy alegre y **divertido**. Siempre jugamos y hacemos cosas divertidos juntos. Tengo una hermanita pequeña. Se llama Violeta. Yo la cuido ya que soy el hermano mayor. Es mi **trabajo** cuidar de mi hermanita todo el tiempo.

Ambos vamos a la escuela. Yo estoy en el cuatro año de **primaria**. Mi hermana está en el segundo año. Ella tiene ocho años. Todos los días, caminamos juntos a la escuela. Nuestra escuela está en el mismo **vecindario** donde vivimos. No está lejos. También caminamos con otros compañeros. En total, caminamos cinco o seis compañeros. Algunas veces, somos hasta diez o doce amigos juntos. Es muy divertido estar todos **juntos**. Bromeamos todo el tiempo.

Me gusta ir a la escuela. Todos los días aprendemos algo nuevo.
Tenemos dos profesores. Nuestra **maestra** se llama Carmen. Con ella estudiamos matemáticas, ciencias naturales, lenguaje, y estudios sociales. No pasamos toda la mañana con sumas y restas, pero **estudiando** plantas y animales, aprendiendo sobre nuestro país, y aprendiendo muchas **palabras** nuevas.

El otro maestro que tenemos se llama Raúl. Con él aprendemos sobre **computadoras**. Él nos enseña mucho sobre tecnología y trabajos manuales. Es muy

mom in the world. My father's name is Francisco. It is very cheerful and **fun**. We always play and do fun things together. I have a little sister. She's named Violeta. I take care of her since I am the oldest brother. It's my **job** to take care of my little sister all the time.

We both go to school. I am in the fourth year of **primary** school. My sister is in the second year. She is eight years. Every day, we walk to school together. Our school is in the same **neighborhood** where we live. It is not far. We also walked with other colleagues. In total, we walked five or six companions. Sometimes we are up to ten or twelve friends together.
It's a lot of fun being all **together**. We joke all the time.

I like going to school. Every day we learn something new. We have two teachers. Our **teacher** is called Carmen. With her, we study math, science, language, and social studies. We do not spend all morning with addition and subtraction, but **studying** plants and animals, learning about our country, and learning many new **words**.

The other teacher we have is called Raúl. With him, we learn about **computers**. He teaches us a lot about technology and crafts. He is

creativo. Siempre nos enseña cosas muy prácticas. Me encantan los **proyectos** que hacemos con él.

La única cosa de la escuela que no me gusta es los **exámenes**. Todos los meses tenemos exámenes. No me gustan porque me pongo **nervioso**. Todos mis amigos me dicen que todo está bien. Pero no puedo. Siempre me pongo muy **preocupado**. Pero, trato de pensar positivamente. Al final, siempre tengo buenas notas. Mis amigos me dicen que soy buen **estudiante**. Creo que sí. Siempre gano todas mis materias.

Me encanta la escuela. Quiero ser **astronauta**. Sé que eso requiere mucho estudio. No importa porque me encanta estudiar. La mejor parte de todo es que tengo muchos amigos. Ellos me motivan a estudiar. Mi hermanita también es buena estudiante. Ella es la mejor de su clase. Ella quiere ser doctora. Ella es muy **inteligente** y **talentosa**.

Y tú, ¿te gusta la escuela?

¿Cuál es tu clase favorita?

Mi clase favorita es ciencias naturales. Me fascina estudiar sobre el espacio. Me encanta **aprender** sobre los planetas y las estrellas. Es una materia tan interesante. Trato de aprender todo sobre el **espacio**. Por eso

very **creative**. He always teaches us very practical things. I love the **projects** we do with him.

The only thing about the school that I don't like is the **exams**. Every month we have exams. I don't like them because I get **nervous**. All my friends tell me that everything is fine. But I cannot. I always get very **worried**. But I try to think positively. In the end, I always get good grades. My friends tell me that I am a good **student**. I think so. I always win all my subjects.

I love school. I want to be an **astronaut**. I know that requires a lot of studies. It doesn't matter because I love studying. The best part of all is that I have a lot of friends. They motivate me to study. My little sister is also a good student. She is the best in her class. She wants to be a doctor.

She is very **smart** and **talented**. And you, do you like school?

What is your favorite class?

My favorite class is natural sciences. I am fascinated by the study of space. I love **learning** about planets and stars. It is such an interesting subject. I try to learn everything about **space**.

That's why I want to be an astronaut. I want to travel to very

quiero ser astronauta. Quiero viajar a planetas muy lejanos. Quiero conocer a personas de otros **planetas**. Quiero hacer amigos **extraterrestres**. ¡Quiero vivir en otro planeta! Es una idea tan genial vivir en otro planeta.	distant planets. I want to meet people from other **planets**. I want to make **extraterrestrial** friends. I want to live on another planet! It's such a cool idea to live on another planet.

El presente simple (The present simple)

In Spanish, the present simple is used to describe the routine actions and characteristics of people and objects. In this story, the main character is describing himself and the things he usually does. So, you can see how he tells you about who he is and the various things he does.

For example, the statement, "me llamo José" (my name is José) is a great example of using the verb "llamar" to tell you about his name. As such, you can find out about his personal information. Also, he mentions, "vivo en una ciudad muy grande" (I live in a very big city). In this example, the character is telling you about his life.

Now, it's important to remember that you can use the present simple to describe characteristics that are permanent states. This is the same function as the verb "ser." So, you can use the present simple to talk about you, your family, and your life.

Let's take a look at some more examples:
- Tengo nueve años. (I am nine years old.)
- Vivo en una aldea. (I live in a village.)
- Voy a un colegio muy bonito. (I go to a very nice school.)
- Trabajo en una fábrica de automóviles. (I work in an automobile factory.)
- Estudio medicina en la universidad. (I study medicine at the university.)

In these examples, you can see how the present simple is used to

talk about personal information. So, you can provide information about yourself by using these verbs:
- Tener (to have)
- Vivir (to live)
- Ir (to go)
- Trabajar (to work)
- Estudiar (to study)

Please note that "tener" and "ir" are irregular. So, their structure is different from the conjugation patterns we discussed earlier. Let's take a look at some examples of their conjugation in the present simple.

Tener
- Yo **tengo** una bebida caliente. (I have a hot drink.)
- Tú **tienes** una vieja camisa. (You have an old shirt.)
- Él **tiene** muchas revistas sobre autos. (He has many magazines about cars.)
- Ella **tiene** muchos juguetes de madera. (She has many wooden toys.)
- Nosotros **temenos** poco tiempo. (We have little time.)
- Vosotros **tenéis** amigos aburridos. (You have boring friends.)
- Ellos **tienen** unos cuantos libros. (They have some books.)
- Ellas **tienen** una lista de compras. (They have a shopping list.)

As you can see, "tener" is irregular as its conjugation does not follow the traditional pattern we discussed earlier.

Now, let's take a look at "ir."

Ir
- Yo **voy** al cine con frecuencia. (I go frequently go to the movies.)
- Tú **vas** al banco una vez por semana. (You go to the bank once a week.)
- Él **va** con el dentista una vez al año. (He goes to the dentist once a year.)
- Ella **va** con su abuelita. (She goes with her grandmother.)
- Nosotros **vamos** con la policía. (We go to the police.)
- Vosotros **vais** solos. (You go alone.)
- Ellos **van** acompañados. (They go together.)

- Ellas **van** con sus primos. (They go with their cousins.)

Please keep in mind the irregular conjugation of "Ir." Once you get the hang of it, it's quite easy to remember.

Also, please don't forget that we can omit the subject in these sentences. So, "Yo voy al cine con frecuencia" could also be, "voy al cine con frecuencia." Please don't forget it!

You can also use the present simple to talk about your routine activities. Here are some examples.
- Trabajo en una fábrica de automóviles todos los días. (I work at an automobile factory every day.)
- Él come pollo todas las noches. (He eats chicken every evening.)
- Nosotros jugamos fútbol por la noche. (We play soccer at night.)
- Ellas ven documentales sobre animales. (They watch documentaries about animals.)
- Tú cocinas los fines de semana. (You cook on the weekends.)

As you can see, these are all examples of routine activities. You can say the time when they happen, or not. It depends on what you want to say. Please remember these are activities you do all the time. These are not activities that you are doing at this moment.

Acertijos (Riddles)

Ejercicio número uno (exercise number one):

Coloca las palabras en el orden correcto. (Put the words in the right order).

a. niños / juegan / Los / fútbol / escuela / la / en

_____

b. trabajan / en / Ellos / granja / una

_____

c. ladra / noche / perro / El / la / en

_____

d. auto / va / calle / por / El / la

_____

Ejercicio número dos (exercise number two):
Escoge la respuesta correcta. (Choose the right answer).
1. Jorge_____a practicar volibol por la tarde (va / van / vas)
2. María_____un nuevo moño en su cabello (tengo / tienes / tiene)
3. Los amigos_____a jugar ajedrez. (va / van / vas)
4. Ellos_____muchos libros sobre el espacio. (tengo / tienen / tiene)
5. Ellas_____al veterinario con su mascota. (va / van / vas)

Soluciones (Solutions)

Ejercicio número uno (exercise number one):
Coloca las palabras en el orden correcto. (Put the words in the right order.)
1. niños / juegan / Los / fútbol / escuela / la / en

   Los niños juegan fútbol en la escuela.

2. trabajan / en / Ellos / granja / una

   Ellos trabajan en una granja.

3. ladra / noche / perro / El / la / en

   El perro ladra en la noche.

4. auto / va / calle / por / El / la

   El auto va por la calle.

Ejercicio número dos (exercise number two):
Escoge la respuesta correcta. (Choose the right answer)
1. Jorge_____a practicar volibol por la tarde (**va** / van / vas)
2. María_____un nuevo moño en su cabello (tengo /

tienes / **tiene**)
3. Los amigos_____a jugar ajedrez. (va / **van** / vas)
4. Ellos _____muchos libros sobre el espacio. (tengo /**tienen** / tiene)
5. Ellas_al veterinario con su mascota. (va / **van** / vas)

Chapter 12
Capítulo Doce

Estoy Leyendo un Libro

Important words to remember

Español	English	Pronunciation
leer	Read	/leh – her/
historietas	comics	/eehs – toh – reeh – eh – tahs/
libros	books	/leeh – brohs/
librerías	bookstores	/leeh – breh – reeh – ahs/
ilustraciones	illustrations	/eeh – loohs – trah – seeh – oh –nehs/
lindos	cute	/leehn – dohs/
estrellas	stars	/ehs – treh – yahs/
lejanos	distant	/leh – hah – nohs/
maravilloso	marvelous	/mah – rah – veeh – yoh – soh/
información	information	/eehn – fohr – mah – seeh – ohn/
galaxias	galaxies	/gah – lahk – seeh – ahs/
caballeros	knights	/kah – bah – yeh – rohs/
dragones	dragons	/drah – goh – nehs/
valientes	brave	/vah – leeh – ehn – tehs/
algo	something	/ahl – goh/
mundo	world	/moohn – doh/
reto	challenge	/reh – toh/

próximo	next	/prohk – seeh – moh/
fabuloso por	fabulous	/fah – booh – loh – soh/
favor	please	/porh – fah – vohr/
imaginando	imagining	/eeh – mah – heeh – nahn - doh/
escondido	hidden	/ehs – kohn – deeh – doh/
también	too	/tahm – beeh – ehn/

Estoy Leyendo un Libro (I Am Reading a Book)

Español	English
Hola, me llamo Carmen. Tengo once años. Me encanta **leer**. Me gusta leer toda clase de libros. Soy aficionada a las **historietas**. Pero en realidad, me encantan todos los libros. Me fascina leer cualquier cosa. Por eso, mi padre me compra todos los **libros** que quiero. Él no se molesta cuando le pido dinero para libros. Él siempre está dispuesto a comprarme los libros que quiero. Usualmente, me lleva a las **librerías**. Ahí hay toda clase de libros. Siempre tenemos mucho de dónde escoger. Ahora, estoy leyendo un libro sobre animales. Este libro es muy bueno porque tiene muchas **ilustraciones**. Contiene explicaciones sobre cada animal, lo que come, donde vive, y lo que necesita para estar bien. De todos los animales, me encantan los caballos. Son animales más	Hello, my name is Carmen. I am eleven years old. I love **reading**. I like to read all kinds of books. I am fond of **comics**. But actually, I love all the books. I love reading anything. So, my father buys me all the **books** I want. He doesn't mind when I ask him for money for books. He is always willing to buy me the books I want. Usually, he takes me to **bookstores**. There are all kinds of books there. We always have a lot to choose from. Now, I am reading a book about animals. This book is very good because it has a lot of **illustrations**. It contains explanations about each animal, what it eats, where it lives, and what it needs to be well. Of all the animals, I love horses. They are the **cutest** animals.

lindos.

También estoy leyendo un libro sobre el espacio. Estoy fascinada con las **estrellas**. Me gustaría viajar al especio algún día. Creo que sería algo genial viajar a planetas **lejanos**. Sería **maravilloso** hablar con personas de otros planetas.

En este momento, estamos estudiando el espacio en mi clase. Es algo maravilloso. Lo mejor es que hay mucha **información** sobre el espacio en el internet.

Estoy guardando toda la información que encuentro. Mi hermano me está ayudando a encontrar más información. Nos pasamos horas buscando información sobre planetas y **galaxias**.

Mi hermano está escribiendo un libro. Creo que es genial. Es una historia sobre **caballeros** y **dragones**. Yo estoy leyendo la primera parte del libro. En esta parte, el héroe está peleando contra los dragones. Los dragones están atacando a la ciudad. Pero los caballeros están defendiendo a las personas. Me parece genial cómo los dragones no pueden vencer contra los **valientes** caballeros.

Y tú, ¿estás leyendo algún libro?

Espero que sí. Leer es algo maravilloso. Leer me

I am also reading a book about space. I am fascinated by the **stars**. I would like to travel to space one day. I think it would be a great thing to travel to **distant** planets. It would be **wonderful** to talk to people from other planets.

Right now, we are studying space in my class. It is something wonderful. The best thing is that there is a lot of **information** about the space on the internet. I am saving all the information I find. My brother is helping me find more information. We spend hours looking for information about planets and **galaxies**.

My brother is writing a book. I think it's great. It is a story about **knights** and **dragons**. I am reading the first part of the book. In this part, the hero is fighting dragons. The dragons are attacking the city. But the knights are defending the people. It seems great to me how dragons cannot win against **brave** knights.

And you, are you reading a book?

I hope so. Reading is a wonderful thing. Reading is

está ayudando a aprender cosas	helping me learn new things. When I learn **something** new, I am happy to
nuevas. Cuando aprendo **algo** nuevo, me siento feliz de encontrar un mundo nuevo lleno de ideas y de aventuras. Estoy descubriendo nuevas formas de ver el **mundo**. Creo que esto es fascinante. Espero que tú también.	find a new world full of ideas and adventures. I am discovering new ways of seeing the **world**. I think this is fascinating. I hope you too.

    Mis amigos y yo estamos haciendo un **reto**. El reto consiste en termina un libro por mes. Yo estoy terminando el libro de los animales. El **próximo** mes tenemos un libro sobre el polo norte. Es una novela en donde los personajes están viajando al polo norte. Se ve que es **fabuloso**. Ya lo quiero empezar. Pero primero debo terminar el libro que estoy leyendo en este momento.

    Si me quieres recomendar un libro, **por favor** hazlo. Creo que los libros tienen tantas cosas maravillosas por descubrir. Lo podemos descubrir juntos.

    Siempre que leo me estoy **imaginando** el mundo de los personajes del libro. Es algo tan maravilloso estar en ese mundo. Todas las personas deben leer.

    My friends and I are doing a challenge. The **challenge** is to finish one book per month. I am finishing the book about animals. **Next** month, we have a book on the North Pole. It is a novel where the characters are traveling to the North Pole. It looks like it's **fabulous**. I want to start it. But first I must finish the book that I am reading right now.

    If you want to recommend a book to me, **please** do so. I think books have so many wonderful things to discover. We can discover it together.

    Whenever I read, I am **imagining** the world of the characters in the book. It is such a wonderful thing to be in that world. All people must read.

Así, todos pueden encontrar un mundo **escondido** dentro de las páginas de un libro. Muchas veces, no se ve por la portada. Pero cuando lees, encuentras algo tan especial. Esos son los libros para mí, algo lindo y especial. Espero que tú **también**.	Thus, everyone can find a world **hidden** within the pages of a book. Many times, it is not seen through the cover. But when you read, you find something so special. Those are the books for me, something nice and special. I hope you, **too**.

El present continuo (The present continuous)

In Spanish, the present continuous works much the way it does in English. As such, it is easy to compare. Generally speaking, the present continuous is used to talk about actions that are currently in progress or that are temporary.

In the story, we see the main character talk about the books she is currently reading. She uses phrases such as, "estoy leyendo un libro sobre animales" (I am reading a book about animals.)

In this example, we can see that this is an action she is doing at this time. While she is not actually reading the book at the time of speaking, it is an action she is doing at present. Also, the main character is making it clear that the action is in progress at the time of speaking.

Here is another example:

"En este momento, estamos estudiando el espacio en mi clase" (At this moment, we are studying about space is my class.)

In this example, the character is telling us about a temporary action. So, it is something that's happening now but will be over soon. As such, it is not a permanent action. To make the present continuous, you need the verb "estar" plus a verb in the gerund form. The gerund form in Spanish refers to the -ando and -endo endings. So, you need to change the verb ending to make the corresponding change. The -ando and -endo endings are the same as the ING ending in English.

Let's take a look at a couple of examples:

- Tina está comiendo un helado. (Tina is eating an ice cream.)
- Diego está bailando con su hermana. (Diego is dancing with his sister.)
- Roberto y María están hacienda ejercicio. (Roberto and María

are doing exercise.)
- Dora y yo estamos viendo un documental. (Dora and I are watching a documentary.)
- Ellos están leyendo esto. (They are reading this.)

To conjugate the present continuous, please don't forget the proper conjugation of the verb "estar." Please take a minute to review it in case you need some extra practice. It will help you get the right sentence formation.

Here is a formula to help you remember.

Subject + estar + verb (-ando / - endo)

Let's break down an example

Juan está haciendo tareas. (Juan is doing homework.)

Subject = Juan Estar = está Verb = haciendo Complement = tareas

With this formula, you will always get it right. So, please take a minute to review it. That way, you'll know exactly what to do the next time you need to use the present continuous.

Acertijos (Riddles)

Ejercicio número uno (exercise number one):

Por Favor escoja la respuesta correcta. (Please choose the correct answer.)

1. Franco_____jugando a los bolos.
    a. Están
    b. Está
    c. Estamos
2. Patricia está_____una pera jugosa.
    a. Comer
    b. Comería
    c. Comiendo
3. Yo_____estudiando mis clases de español.
    a. Estoy
    b. Estamos

        c. Está
4. Los gatos _____durmiendo.
        a. Está
        b. Están
        c. Estamos
5. Miguel está_____su cumpleaños.
        a. Celebrando
        b. Celebrar
        c. celebré

Ejercicio número dos (exercise number two):
Combine la forma correcta del verbo con su gerundio. (Match the correct form of the verb with its gerund.)

Comer	durmiendo
Jugar	conociendo
Ir	comiendo
Viajar	jugando
Dormir	viajando
conocer	yendo

Soluciones (Solutions)

Ejercicio número uno (exercise number one):
Por Favor escoja la respuesta correcta. (Please choose the correct answer.)
1. Franco_____jugando a los bolos.
    a. Están
    b. Está
    c. Estamos
2. Patricia está_____una pera jugosa.
    a. Comer
    b. Comería
    c. Comiendo
3. Yo _____estudiando mis clases de español.

105

a. Estoy
   b. Estamos
   c. Está
4. Los gatos ____durmiendo.
   a. Está
   b. Están
   c. Estamos
5. Miguel está_____su cumpleaños.
   a. Celebrando
   b. Celebrar
   c. Celebré

Ejercicio número dos (exercise number two):

Combine la forma correcta del verbo con su gerundio. (Match the correct form of the verb with its gerund.)

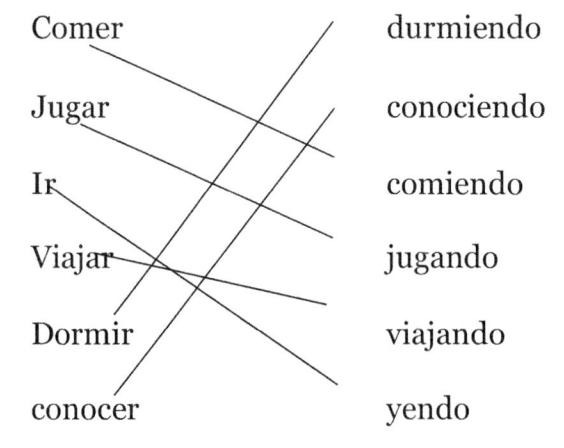

Comer	durmiendo
Jugar	conociendo
Ir	comiendo
Viajar	jugando
Dormir	viajando
conocer	yendo

Chapter 13
Capítulo Trece

Mi Cumpleaños Fue Ayer

Important words to remember

Español	English	Pronunciation
feliz	happy	/feh – leehz/
fiesta	party	/feeh – ehs- tah/
genial	cool	/heh – neeh – ahl/
obsequio	gift	/ohb – seh – keeh – oh/
chaqueta	jacket	/chah – keh – tah/
especiales	special	/ehs – peh – seeh – ah – lehs/
dinosaurio	dinosaur	/deeh – noh – sahw – reeh –oh/
dulces	sweets	/doohl – sehs/
año	year	/ahn – yoh/
sorpresa	surprise	/sohr – preh – sah/
hamburguesas	hamburgers	/ahm – boohr - geh – sas/
refresco	drinks	/reh – frehs – koh/
delicioso	delicious	/deh – leeh – seeh – oh – soh/
comer	eat	/kohn – mehr/
vainilla	vanilla	/vahy – neeh – yah/
jamás	never	/hah – mahs/
impresionados	impressed	/eehm – preh – seeh – oh – nah– dos/

108

definitivamente	efinitely	/deh – feeh – neeh – teeh – vah– mehn – teh/
mesa	table	/meh – sah/
cantar	sing	/kahn – tahr/
canción	songs	/kahn – seeh – ohn/
recuerdo	souvenir	/reh – kooh – ehr – doh/
alucinante	awesome	/ah – looh – seeh – nahn – teh/
experiencia	experience	/ehks – peh – reeh – ehn – sah/
excepcional	exceptional	/eks – sehp – seeh – oh – nahl/
afortunado	lucky	/ah – fohr – tooh – nah – doh/
cumpleaños	birthday	/kooh – pleh – ahn – yohs/
rebanada	slice	/reh – bah – nah – dah/
trozo	piece	/troh – zoh/

Mi Cumpleaños Fue Ayer (My Birthday Was Yesterday)

Español	English
Hola, soy Miguel. Tengo diez años. Bueno, acabo de cumplir diez. Tuve nueve años. Ahora tengo diez. Estoy muy **feliz** porque ayer fue mi fiesta de cumpleaños. Me emocionó muchísimo mi fiesta. Fue la mejor **fiesta** del mundo. Todo el mundo estuvo ahí. Estuvieron mis padres, mis hermanos, mis primos, y mis compañeros del colegio. Todos se la pasaron **genial** junto conmigo.	Hello, I'm Miguel. I am ten years old. Well, I just turned ten. I was nine years old. Now I have ten. I am very happy because yesterday was my birthday party. I was very excited about my party. It was the best party in the world. Everybody was there. There were my parents, my brothers, my cousins, and my classmates. Everyone had a great time with me.
Todo comenzó cuando mis padres me dieron un **obsequio** muy especial. Ellos me dieron una **chaqueta** con mi nombre. Esta era la chaqueta del cumpleañero. Solo yo la tuve porque era mi fiesta. Así, todos los chicos supieron que yo era el cumpleañero. Fue algo genial. Mis padres son tan **especiales** conmigo.	It all started when my parents gave me a very special gift. They gave me a jacket with my name on it. This was the birthday boy's jacket. I only had it because it was my party. So, all the boys knew that I was the birthday boy. It was cool. My parents are so special to me.
Luego, hicimos la piñata. La piñata estuvo hecha en forma de **dinosaurio**. Mis padres saben que me encantan los dinosaurios. Pero la piñata no estuvo llena de **dulces**; ¡estuvo llena solo de chocolates! Todos mis amigos tuvimos muchos chocolates. Creo que ahora tenemos chocolates para todo un **año**. Fue una **sorpresa** tan genial. Nunca vi una piñata llena solo de chocolates.	Then we made the piñata. The piñata was made in the shape of a dinosaur. My parents know that I love dinosaurs. But the piñata was not full of sweets. It was filled with only chocolates! All my friends had a lot of chocolates. I think we now have chocolates for a whole year. It was such a great surprise. I never saw a piñata filled with only chocolates.
Después de la piñata, comimos mucho. Comimos **hamburguesas**	After the piñata, we ate a lot.

con papas fritas. Me encantó comer mi comida favorita. Tomamos **refresco** de naranja. Me comí dos hamburguesas. Nunca pensé comer tanto. Pero valió la pena. Estuvo **delicioso**. Mis amigos se terminaron toda la comida. No quedó absolutamente nada de comer. Mis padres se sorprendieron de vernos **comer** tanto.

Lo mejor de la fiesta fue el pastel. El pastel era de **vainilla** y en forma de nave espacial. ¡No lo pude creer! **Jamás** vi un pastel en forma de nave espacial. Era tan genial. Todos fueron **impresionados** con este pastel tan increíble.
Definitivamente, fue de lo mejor.

Mis padres colocaron el pastel en el centro de la **mesa**. Todos hicieron una rueda para cantar "feliz cumpleaños." Mis padres comenzaron la canción. Pronto, todos comenzaron a **cantar**.
Cantamos en coro. Una vez terminaron la **canción**, contaron uno, dos, tres, cuatro, cinco, seis, siete, ocho, nueve... y ¡diez! Ahora tengo diez años. Ya no tengo nueve. Ahora tengo diez años.

Todos mis amigos me dejaron un regalito. Ellos son tan especiales. No fueron cosas muy caras. Pero eso no importa. Lo que importa es que

We ate hamburgers with fries. I loved eating my favorite food. We took orange soda. I had two hamburgers. I never thought to eat that much. But it was worth it. It was delicious. My friends finished all the food. There was absolutely nothing left to eat. My parents were surprised to see us eat so much.

The best thing about the party was the cake. The cake was vanilla and in the shape of a spaceship. I cannot believe it! I never saw a spaceship cake. It was so cool. Everyone was impressed with this amazing cake. It was definitely the best.

My parents placed the cake in the center of the table. They all made a wheel to sing "happy birthday." My parents started the song.
Soon, everyone began to sing. We sing in a chorus. Once they finished the song, they counted one, two, three, four, five, six, seven, eight, nine... and ten! Now I am ten years old. I don't have nine anymore. Now I am ten years old.

All my friends left me a gift. They are so special. They were not very expensive things. But that

mis amigos me dieron algo muy valioso. Guardo todos mis regalos como tesoros. Son el **recuerdo** de una fiesta **alucinante**. Todos comimos mucho pastel. Fue la mejor **experiencia** de mi vida. El pastel fue la estrella de la fiesta. Todos se quedaron encantados con el pastel. No puedo creer la fiesta tan **excepcional** que tuve. Ahora, debo esperar un año entero para mi próxima fiesta. No importa. Estoy tan feliz. Soy un chico muy **afortunado**. Y tú, ¿Cuándo es tu **cumpleaños**? Espero me invites a tu fiesta. Por favor guárdame una **rebanada** de	does not matter. What matters is that my friends gave me something very valuable. I keep all my gifts as treasures. They are the memory of an amazing party. We all ate a lot of cake. It was the best experience of my life. The cake was the star of the party. Everyone was delighted with the cake. I can't believe what an exceptional party I had. Now, I have to wait a whole year for my next party. Never mind. I'm so happy. I am a very lucky boy. And you, when is your birthday? I hope you invite me to your party. Please save me a slice of
pastel. No importa qué tipo de pastel es. Solamente guarda un **trozo** para tu amigo Miguel. Estoy seguro de visitarte para tu fiesta. ¿Sabes lo mejor? Te llevaré un regalo muy especial de todo corazón.	cake. It doesn't matter what kind of cake it is. Just save a piece for your friend Miguel. I am sure to visit you at your party. Do you know the best? I will bring you a very special gift with all my heart.

El pretérito perfecto simple (The past simple)

The past simple is essentially used to talk about any action that occurred at any point in the past. The actions are finished and are not in progress in the present. So, you can use the past simple any time you want to talk about something you did at some point in the past.

Also, you will notice that the verb endings change for the

conjugation. Please check out Chapter 2 to review the verb endings used in the past simple. Practice will help you improve your overall grammar skills. So, the more practice you get, the better you will become.

Let's take a look at some examples:

In this story, the main character is talking about his birthday party. He says the following:

"Fue la mejor fiesta del mundo." (It was the best past in the world.)

This example uses the past tense of the verb "ser" to describe his party. Also, please notice that he did not use a subject at the beginning of this phrase as it is clear from the context that he is talking about his birthday party.

Here is another example.

"Mis padres colocaron el pastel en el centro de la mesa." (My parents placed the cake at the center of the table.)

In this example, the verb "colocaron" is the past of "colocar" (to place). It agrees with the subject "mis padres" (my parents).

Let's look at a few more examples of the past simple tense:

- Juan **jugó** con su mascota. (Juan played with his pet.)
- Amanda y Tania **caminaron** a su escuela esta mañana. (Amanda and Tania walked to their school this morning.)
- Pedro **compró** una nueva historieta el fin de semana. (Pedro bought a new comic on the weekend.)
- Yo trabajé **mucho** con mis amigos. (I worked a lot with my friends.)
- Los hermanos **hicieron** mucho por su comunidad. (The brothers did a lot for their community.)

In all of these examples, we can see how the verb changes according to the subject. So, please review the verb endings. They will help you to get the right conjugation every time!

Acertijos (Riddles)

Ejercicio número uno (exercise number one):

Cambia las frases de presente a pasado. (Change the phrases from present to past.)

1. Yo juego con mis amigos en mi casa.

2. Ella hace ricos pasteles el fin de semana.

3. Pablo viaja cada verano con su familia.

4. La maestra tiene muchos marcadores.

5. El perro come un pequeño hueso.

Ejercicio número dos (exercise number two):
Coloca las frases en el orden correcto. (Place the sentences in the correct order.)
1. tenis / Pablo / jugaron / y / Miguel

2. trabajé / Yo / una / oficina / en

3. fueron / estudiantes / una / excursión / Los / a

4. botones / madre / los / Mi / arregló

5. increíble / fue / viaje / El

Soluciones (Solutions)

Ejercicio número uno (exercise number one):
Cambia las frases de presente a pasado. (Change the phrases from present to past.)

1. Yo juego con mis amigos en mi casa.
Yo jugué con mis amigos en casa.

2. Ella hace ricos pasteles el fin de semana.
Ella hizo ricos pasteles el fin de semana.

3. Pablo viaja cada verano con su familia.
Pablo viajó cada verano con su con su familia.

4. La maestra tiene muchos marcadores.
La maestra tuvo muchos marcadores.

5. El perro come un pequeño hueso.
El perro comió un pequeño hueso.

Ejercicio número dos (exercise number two):
Coloca las frases en el orden correcto. (Place the sentences in the correct order.)

6. tenis / Pablo / jugaron / y / Miguel

Miguel y Pablo jugaron tenis.

7. trabajé / Yo / una / oficina / en

Yo trabajé en una oficina.

8. fueron / estudiantes / una / excursión / Los / a

Los estudiantes fueron a una excursión.

9. botones / madre / los / Mi / arregló

Mi madre arregló los botones.

10. increíble / fue / viaje / El

El viaje fue increíble.

Chapter 14
Capítulo Catorce

Tuvimos Unas Grandes Vacaciones

Important words to remember:

Español	English	Pronunciation
vacaciones	vacation	/vah – kah – seeh – oh – nehs/
viaje	travel	/veeh – ah – heh/
playa	beach	/plah – yah/
surfear	surf	/surh – feeh – ahr/
nadar	swim	/nah – dahr/
arena	sand	/ah – reh – nah/
calor	heat	/kah – lohr/
montañas	mountains	/mohn – tahn- yahs/
vista	view	/veehs – tah/
pájaros	birds	/pah – hah – rohs/
bosque	forest	/bohs – keh/
fogata	bonfire	/foh – gah – tah/
casa de campaña	tent	/kah – sah – deh – kahm – pahn– yah/
conejos	rabbits	/koh – neh – hohs/
ardillas	squirrels	/ahr – deeh – yahs/
malvaviscos	marshmallows	/mahl – vah – veehs – kohs/

Spanish	English	Pronunciation
sopa	soup	/soh – pah/
teléfonos celulares	cellphone	/teh – leh – foh – nohs - seh –looh – lah – rehs/
jugar	play	/hooh – gahr/
videojuegos	videogames	/veeh – deeh – oh – hooh – eh –gohs/
patio	yard	/pah – teeh – oh/
inolvidables	unforgettable	/eehn – ohl – veeh – dah – blehs/
invitar	invite	/eehn – veeh – tahr/
bailamos	dance	/bah – eeh – lah – mohs/
libertad	freedom	/leeh – behr – tahd/
planificando	planning	/plah – neeh – feeh – kahn – doh/
problema	problem	/proh – bleh – mah/

Tuvimos Unas Grandes Vacaciones (We Had a Great Vacation)

Español	English
¡Mis últimas **vacaciones** fueron geniales!	My last vacation was great!
Nos fuimos de **viaje** con mi familia a diferentes lugares. El primer lugar que visitamos fue la playa. La **playa** estuvo maravillosa. Las olas estaban fuertes. Me encantó porque pudimos surfear. Llevaba mi tabla	We went on a **trip** with my family to different places. The first place we visited was the beach. The **beach** was wonderful. The waves were strong. I loved it because we were able to surf. I carried my

conmigo. Entonces, mis hermanas y yo nos metimos al agua. Pasamos un día entero surfeando. Creo que no comimos de la emoción.

Surfear es mi deporte favorito. A mis hermanas también les gusta. Pero ellas prefieren **nadar**.

Estuvimos cuatro días en la playa. Todos los días jugábamos en la **arena**. Corríamos como locos con nuestro perro Rocky. Rocky disfruta muchísimo el agua. Pasó metido en el agua todo el tiempo. Creo que él pasó más tiempo dentro del agua que nosotros. En verdad pienso que Rocky disfrutó muchísimo estar en playa. Hacía mucho **calor**. Pienso que por eso Rocky estaba tan feliz de meterse al agua.

Después de unos días en playa, mi padre decidió cambiar. Entonces, nos fuimos a unas **montañas** cercanas. En estas montañas, se puede ver la playa desde lo alto. Es una **vista** increíble. Lo mejor de todo es que es tan tranquilo.

Solamente se oyen los **pájaros** cantar. Es un lugar muy lindo.

Acá, cambiamos de actividades. Ahora ya no corríamos en la arena. Ahora, nuestras actividades estaban en el **bosque**. Íbamos a caminar, hicimos una gran **fogata**, y construimos una **casa de campaña**. Rocky también disfrutó mucho estar en el bosque.

board with me. So, my sisters and I went into the water. We spent a whole day **surfing**. I don't think we ate out of emotion. Surfing is my favorite sport. My sisters like it too. But they prefer to **swim**.

We were on the beach for four days. Every day, we played in the **sand**. We were running like crazy with our dog Rocky. Rocky really enjoys the water. He was in the water the whole time. I think he spent more time in the water than we did. I really think Rocky really enjoyed being at the beach. It was very **hot**. I think that's why Rocky was so happy to get in the water.

After a few days on the beach, my father decided to change. So, we went to some nearby **mountains**. In these mountains, you can see the beach from above. It is an incredible sight. Best of all, it is so peaceful. Only the **birds** sing. It is a very nice place.

Here, we changed activities. Now, we were no longer running in the sand. Now our activities were in the **forest**. We went for a walk, made a big fire, and built a **tent**. Rocky also really enjoyed being in the woods. We ran after some animals like **rabbits** and

Corríamos detrás de algunos animalitos como **conejos** y **ardillas**. Nunca las alcanzamos. Pero fue divertido jugar con todos los animalitos del bosque.

En las noches, cocinábamos **malvaviscos** en la fogata. Hicimos comida deliciosa como hamburguesas y **sopa**. Lo mejor de todo fue estar al aire libre sin el ruido de la ciudad. Debido a nuestra ubicación, nuestros **teléfonos celulares** no funcionaban. Entonces, no podíamos hacer nada más que **jugar**, hablar, y disfrutar de la compañía en familia.

Definitivamente, fue una experiencia maravillosa.

Pasamos tres días en el bosque. Mi madre estaba ansiosa por volver a casa. Mi padre pensó que era una buena idea pasar unos días en casa. Regresamos a casa rápidamente. Mis hermanas y yo nos pasamos el resto de nuestras vacaciones jugando **videojuegos**, corriendo en el **patio** con Rocky, y luego comiendo las comidas deliciosas que preparó mamá.

Fueron días **inolvidables**.

El último día de nuestras

squirrels. We never reach them. But it was fun playing with all the animals in the forest.

In the evenings, we cooked **marshmallows** on the campfire. We made delicious food like burgers and **soup**. Best of all was being outdoors without the noise of the city. Due to our location, our **cell phones** were not working.

So, we could do nothing but **play**, talk, and enjoy the family company. It was definitely a wonderful experience.

We spent three days in the forest. My mother was eager to go home. My father thought it was a good idea to spend a few days at home. We returned home quickly. My sisters and I spent the rest of our vacation playing **video games**, running on the **yard** with Rocky, and then eating the delicious meals Mom made. They were **unforgettable** days.

The last day of our vacation was the best. That day, my father prepared a small party. He allowed us to invite all of our friends. It was the last day before going back to

vacaciones fue el mejor. Ese día, mi padre preparó una pequeña fiesta. Él nos permitió **invitar** a todos nuestros amigos. Fue el último día antes de volver a la escuela. La fiesta estuvo genial. Comimos mucho, jugamos, y **bailamos**. Lastimosamente, era
    nuestro último día de **libertad**. Al día siguiente, debíamos volver a clases. No estaba mal. Pero todos estábamos tristes. No queríamos regresar a clases. Lo único que queríamos eran más vacaciones.

Ahora, debo esperar hasta las próximas vacaciones. Mis hermanas y yo ya estamos **planificando** nuestro próximo viaje. Les diremos a nuestros padres a dónde queremos ir. Creo que esas vacaciones estarán geniales también. Pero, debemos esperar mucho tiempo. Mientras tanto, debemos estudiar mucho. Todos queremos ganar nuestras clases. Lo mejor es estudiar. Así, podemos ganar todas nuestras clases sin **problema**. Creo que este año será muy divertido. Hay muchas cosas por hacer y aprender.

school. The party was cool. We ate a lot, we played, and we **danced**. Unfortunately, it was our last day of **freedom**. The next day, we were to go back to school.

It was not bad. But we were all sad. We didn't want to go back to class. All we wanted was more vacation.

Now, I must wait until the next vacation. My sisters and I are already **planning** our next trip. We will tell our parents where we want to go. I think those vacations will be great too. But we must wait a long time. Meanwhile, we must study hard. We all want to win our classes. The best thing is to study. Thus, we can win all our classes without any **problem**. I think this year will be a lot of fun. There are many things to do and learn.

El pretérito imperfecto (The indefinite past)

The indefinite past is used to talk about actions that were in progress at some point in the past. The action is finished and does not continue in the present. This means the action was happening at the time the speaker is referring to. This means that you don't necessarily need to say when you did or when it occurred.

You can use the indefinite past to talk about something that you were doing at any time in the past. It is often used to describe activities that you were doing on the weekend, on a specific day, or during a longer time frame. For example, you can use it to talk about activities you were doing when you were a small child, at school, or when traveling. However, you can simply state an action that you did in the past without mentioning when it happened.

Let's take a look at some examples for the story:
- Todos los días jugábamos en la arena. (Every day, we played in the sand.)
- En las noches, cocinábamos malvaviscos en la fogata. (At night, we cooked marshmallows in the bonfire.)

In these examples, we can see that these actions were in progress at some point. We can also see that these are actions that the main character is the story is describing their vacation. So, these were actions that took some time to complete.

Let's take a look at some more examples:
- Los niños estudiaban inglés. (The children studied English.)
- Jorge comía muchos dulces. (Jorge ate too many candies.)
- Violeta estaba en clase anoche. (Violeta was in class last night.)
- Nosotros teníamos mucho que hacer. (We had a lot to do.)
- Ellos compraban refrescos en la tienda. (They bought sodas at the store.)

With these examples, you can now use the indefinite past to talk about the actions that you did at some point in the past whether you indicate the specific time they happened or not. So, do take the time to go over the examples. Please remember that practice makes perfect.

Acertijos (Riddles)

Ejercicio número uno (exercise number one):
Traduce las siguientes frases de español a inglés. (Translate the following sentences from Spanish to English.)
1. Juan y Pedro saltaban en el aire.

2. El oficial de policía dirigía el tráfico.

3. Nosotros jugábamos dominó todos los días.

4. Ellas viajaban cada fin de semana.

5. Martín estudiaba los números en la escuela.

Ejercicio número dos (exercise number two):
Escoge la respuesta correcta. (Choose the right answer.)
1. El gato_____muchos ratones.
    a. Comía
    b. Comieron
    c. Comiste
2. Ángel_____a sus abuelitos.
    a. Visitaban
    b. Visitaba
    c. Visitábamos
3. Mariana___a las estrellas en el cielo.
    a. Mirábamos
    b. Miraban
    c. Miraba
4. Carlos___con sus camiones.
    a. Jugaba
    b. Jugaría
    c. Jugaban
5. Silvia___en una casa pequeña
    a. Vivían
    b. Vivieron
    c. Vivía

Soluciones (Solutions)

Ejercicio número uno (exercise number one):
Traduce las siguientes frases de español a inglés. (Translate the following sentences from Spanish to English.)

1. Juan y Pedro saltaban en el aire.
Juan and Pedro jumped in the air.

2. El oficial de policía dirigía el tráfico.
The police officer directed traffic.

3. Nosotros jugábamos dominó todos los días.
We played dominoes every day.

4. Ellas viajaban cada fin de semana.
They traveled every weekend.

5. Martín estudiaba los números en la escuela.
Martin studied the numbers at school.

Ejercicio número dos (exercise number two):
Escoge la respuesta correcta. (Choose the right answer.)
1. El gato_____muchos ratones.
   a. Comía
   b. Comieron
   c. Comiste
2. Ángel_____a sus abuelitos.
   a. Visitaban
   b. Visitaba
   c. Visitábamos
3. Mariana_____a las estrellas en el cielo.
   a. Mirábamos
   b. Miraban
   c. Miraba
4. Carlos_____con sus camiones.
   a. Jugaba
   b. Jugaría
   c. Jugaban

5. Silvia_____en una casa pequeña
    a. Vivían
    b. Vivieron
    c. Vivía

Chapter 15
Capítulo Quince

Seré un Astronauta

Important words to remember:

Español	English	Pronunciation
sueño	Dream	/sooh – ehn – yoh/
apenas	barely	/ah – peh – nahs/
oportunidad	opportunity	/oh – pohr – tooh – neeh –dahd/
universo	universe	/ooh – neeh – vehr – soh/
preparadas	skilled	/preh – pah – rah - dahs/
ciencias	science	/seeh – ehn – seeh – ahs/
mejor	best	/meh – hohr/
médico	doctor	/meh – deeh – koh/
cirujano	surgeon	/seeh – rooh – hah – noh/
universidad	university	/ooh – neeh – verh – seeh –dahd/
hospital	hospital	/ohs – peeh – tahl/
actriz	actress	/ahk – treehz/
cine	film	/seeh – neh/
televisión	television	/teh – leh – veeh – seeh – ohn/

exitosos	successful	/ehk – seeh – toh – sohs/
orgullosos	proud	/ohr – gooh – yoh – sohs/
razón	right	/rah – zohn/
historia	history	/eehs – toh - reeh – ah/
difícil	tough	/deeh – feeh – seehl/
fácil	easy	/fah – seehl/
único	only	/ooh – neeh – koh/
esfuerzo	effort	/ehs – fooh – ehr – zoh/
dueños	owners	/dooh – ehn – yohs/
futuro	future	/fooh – tooh – roh/
mundo	world	/moohn – doh/

Seré un Astronauta (I Am Going to Be an Astronaut)

Español	English
Tengo un gran **sueño**. Quiero ser astronauta cuando grande. **Apenas** tengo doce años. Pero eso no importa. Pronto tendré la **oportunidad** de estudiar para ser astronauta. Sueño con viajar en el espacio. Sueño con conocer otros planetas y alcanzar las estrellas. Bueno, sé que no es posible estar cerca de una estrella. Pero al menos quiero viajar por todos los rincones del **universo**. Mis padres me dicen que debo	I have a great **dream**. I want to be an astronaut when I grow up. I am **barely** twelve years old. But that does not matter. Soon I will have the **opportunity** to study to be an astronaut. I dream of traveling in space. I dream of meeting other planets and reaching for the stars. Well, I know that it is not possible to be close to a star. But at least I want to travel to all corners of the **universe**. My parents tell me that I should

estudiar mucho. Los astronautas son personas muy inteligentes y **preparadas**. Tendré que estudiar mucho. Tendré que enfocarme en ser buen estudiante. Aprenderé muchas cosas sobre **ciencias** y el espacio.	study hard. Astronauts are very smart and **skilled** people. I will have to study a lot. I will have to focus on being a good student. I will learn a lot about **science** and space.

Mis amigos creen que lo lograré. Ellos me apoyan en mis sueños. Me dan muchos ánimos. Ellos creen que yo seré el **mejor** astronauta del mundo. La verdad, tengo muy buenos amigos. Soy muy afortunado porque ellos siempre me apoyarán en todos mis planes. ¡Qué grandes amigos tengo!

Mis hermanos también me ayudarán a alcanzar mis sueños. Bueno, nos apoyaremos a alcanzar todos nuestros mis sueños. Mi hermano mayor será un gran **médico**. Él sueña como ser un **cirujano**. Él desea estudiar en la **universidad** para luego trabajar en un **hospital**. Creo que lo logrará fácilmente. Mi hermana menor desea ser **actriz**. Es muy buen para actuar. Creo que tendrá mucho éxito en el **cine** o la **televisión**.

Yo estoy convencido que seremos muy **exitosos**. Somos muy unidos y siempre trabajaremos duro por nuestros sueños. Seremos los mejores en todo lo que haremos.

Mis padres estarán muy **orgullosos** de nosotros. De eso estoy seguro.

My friends think I'll make it. They support me in my dreams. They give me a lot of encouragement.

They believe that I will be the **best** astronaut in the world. The truth is, I have very good friends. I am very lucky because they will always support me in all my plans. What great friends I have!

My siblings will also help me achieve my dreams. Well, we will support each other to achieve all our dreams. My older brother will be a great **doctor**. He dreams of being a **surgeon**. He wants to study at the **university** and then work in a **hospital**. I think he will do it easily. My younger sister wants to be an **actress**. He is very good at acting. I think it will be very successful in **film** or **television**.

I am convinced that we will be very **successful**. We are very close and will always work hard for our dreams. We will be the best in everything we do. My parents will be very **proud** of us. I'm sure of that.

The people who support me the most are my teachers. They always

Las personas que más me apoyan son mis maestros. Ellos siempre me dicen que seré un gran astronauta. Ellos creen que llegaré muy lejos. Mis maestros creen que	tell me that I will be a great astronaut. They believe that I will

haré lo necesario para alcanzar mi sueño. La verdad es que tienen **razón**. Haré todo lo necesario para convertirme en el mejor astronauta de la **historia**. Sé que será mucho trabajo, pero no me molesta. Me encantan los retos.

Este será un reto **difícil**, pero lo lograré.

Y tú, ¿Qué serás cuando grande?

Piensa que harás cuando grande. Piensa en tus sueños. Lograrás todo lo que deseas si trabajas y estudias. No será **fácil**, pero con esfuerzo y dedicación, serás el mejor de todos. No importa cuál es tu sueño. Con esfuerzo, serás lo que quieres ser. Tu familia, tus amigos, y tus maestros te ayudarán. Solo tienes que hacer el **mejor esfuerzo posible**.

Yo estoy seguro de que todos haremos lo mejor. Sé que no soy el **único** con grandes sueños. Todos tenemos grandes metas en la vida. Por eso, debemos hacer lo mejor todos los días. Pronto verás el éxito de tus acciones. Si tienes un sueño, debes hacer tu mejor

go very far. My teachers believe that I will do whatever it takes to achieve my dream. The truth is that they are **right**. I will do whatever it takes to become the best astronaut in **history**. I know it will be a lot of work, but it doesn't bother me. I love challenges. This will be a **tough** challenge, but I will make it through.

And you, what will you be when you grow up?

Think about what you will do when you grow up. Think about your dreams. You will achieve everything you want if you work and study. It won't be **easy**, but with effort and dedication, you will be the best of all. It doesn't matter what your dream is. With effort, you will be what you want to be.

Your family, your friends, and your teachers will help you. You just have to do **your best**.

I am sure that we will all do our best. I know I'm not the **only** one with big dreams. We all have big goals in life. Therefore, we must do our best every day. You will soon see the success of your actions. If you have a dream, you should do your

esfuerzo por lograrlo.	**best** to achieve it.
¿Qué esperas?	What are you waiting for?
Empieza hoy a trabajar en tu sueño. Cuando grande, tendrás todo lo que soñaste. ¡Ánimo, tú puedes! Juntos trabajemos y estudiaremos para lograr todos nuestros sueños. Somos los **dueños** del **futuro**.	Start working on your dream today. When you grow up, you will have everything you dreamed of. Let's go, you can do it! Together let's work and study to achieve all our dreams. We are the **owners** of the **future**.
Acompáñame a ser exitosos en la vida. Sé que tienes mucho que aportar al mundo.	Join me to be successful in life. I know you have a lot to contribute to the world.
Juntos haremos un **mundo** mejor.	Together, we will make a better **world**.

El future simple (The future simple)

The future simple is used any time you want to talk about an action that will happen at any point in the future. You don't necessarily need to specify when you think it will happen. All you have to do is use the verb conjugation to indicate that this action will occur in the future.

Let's look at some examples from the story.
- Ellos creen que yo seré el mejor astronauta del mundo. (They believe that I will be the best astronaut in the world.)
- Tus maestros te ayudarán. (Your teachers will help you.)
- Juntos haremos un mundo mejor. (Together, we will make a better world.)

In these examples, we are talking about future actions. However, we are not necessarily saying when the actions will take place. So, please keep this in mind as you don't have to always say when the actions will happen.

Here are some more examples:
- Yo comeré muchas hamburguesas mañana. (I will eat a lot of

hamburgers tomorrow.)
- Él irá a la escuela el domingo. (He will go to school on Sunday.)
- Ellos comprarán una casa nueva. (They will buy a new house.)
- Los perros correrán por todo el patio. (The dogs will run all over the yard.)
- El auto necesitará llantas más grandes. (The car will need bigger tires.)

Acertijos (Riddles)

Ejercicio número uno (exercise number one):
Completa las siguientes frases utilizando el futuro simple. (Complete the following phrases using the future simple.)

1. El próximo año_____.
2. El fin de semana_____.
3. Mis amigos y yo_____.
4. En la escuela_____.
5. En mi próximo cumpleaños_____.

Ejercicio número dos (exercise number two):
Cambia las siguientes frases de presente a futuro. (Change the following phrases from present to future.)

1. Yo juego con mis primos en casa.

_____

2. Ellos comen mucho pastel el fin de semana.

_____

3. Los niños duermen por la noche.

_____

4. Papá arregla el auto por la mañana.

_____

5. Mamá prepara una deliciosa torta.

_____

Soluciones (Solutions)

Ejercicio número uno (exercise number one):
Completa las siguientes frases utilizando el futuro simple. (Complete the following phrases using the future simple.)
Sample answers
1. El próximo *año iré a Europa de vacaciones.*
2. El fin de semana *comeré pizza con mis hermanos.*
3. Mis amigos y yo *jugaremos al fútbol en el parque.*
4. En la escuela *estudiaremos los planetas.*
5. En mi próximo cumpleaños *tendré una fiesta con todos mis amigos.*
6.

Ejercicio número dos (exercise number two):
Cambia las siguientes frases de presente a futuro. (Change the following phrases from present to future.)

1. Yo juego con mis primos en casa.
Yo jugaré con mis primos en casa.

2. Ellos comen mucho pastel el fin de semana.
Ellos comerán mucho pastel el fin de semana.

3. Los niños duermen por la noche.
Los niños dormirán por la noche.

4. Papá arregla el auto por la mañana.
Papá arreglará el auto por la mañana.

5. Mamá prepara una deliciosa torta.
Mamá preparará una deliciosa torta.

Conclusion

We have come to the end of this wonderful journey into the world learning Spanish. We hope you have enjoyed learning about this amazing language. At this point, you have the fundamentals you need to improve your skills. Before you know it, you will be speaking Spanish easily. Best of all, you will be able to understand books, games, movies, and songs in Spanish in no time.

So, what's next?

Please take this opportunity to continue improving your skills. There is so much to learn about the Spanish-speaking world. Spanish is not just about words and grammar. It's about discovering an entirely new culture that's filled with great things and people.

If you are looking to travel, then Spanish will certainly come in handy. When you travel to Spanish-speaking countries, not everyone speaks English. Other times, people speak very basic English. So, it helps to speak Spanish. That way, you won't have trouble communicating with others you meet. This is especially true when you make new friends. The last thing you want is to have trouble talking with your new friends.

Now, please go over any of the lessons you feel you need to review. Keep in mind that practice and repetition are the best ways that you can continue to improve your skills. Practice will help you build on what you have already learned and developed. Over time, focused practice will help you develop amazing Spanish skills.

You'll be surprised to find people envy your ability to learn Spanish so quickly.

Thanks for taking the time to get through all the way to the end of this book. You are surely interested in learning as much as you can about Spanish. This book is just the beginning of this amazing journey. So, be on the lookout for future volumes.

In the meantime, please make every effort to surround yourself with Spanish. You can listen to Spanish songs or watch Spanish TV shows. While they may be a bit tough to understand at first, over time, you'll get the hang of it. The important thing is to practice as much as you can. If you don't practice, then it might be harder for you to learn quickly.

So, what are you waiting for?

Take the time to practice each of the lessons in this book. You will find that the more effort you put into learning Spanish, the faster you will develop your skills in this amazing language. There is no time like the present to learn Spanish. Who knows, it may become very useful for you in the future.

Thanks again.

If you enjoyed this book, please leave a review on Amazon! And then, tell your family, friends, and classmates about it. If they are interested in learning Spanish, they too will find this book to be very useful. Hopefully, they will enjoy learning Spanish as much as you have.

¡Hasta luego!

Printed in Great Britain
by Amazon